SPORTING OREGON

SPORTING OREGON

A PICTORIAL HISTORY OF EARLY OREGON SPORTS

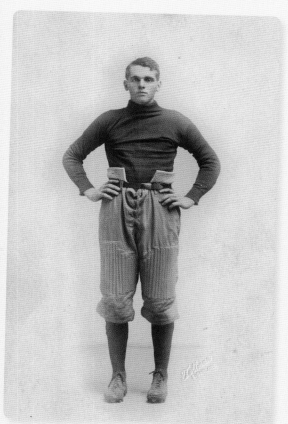

WRITTEN BY AND ILLUSTRATED FROM THE COLLECTION OF **BRIAN S. CAMPF**

OREGON STATE UNIVERSITY PRESS — CORVALLIS

Library of Congress Cataloging-in-Publication Data

Names: Campf, Brian S, author.

Title: Sporting Oregon : a pictorial history of early Oregon sports /
    written by and illustrated from the collection of Brian S. Campf.

Description: Corvallis, OR : Oregon State University Press, 2019. |
    Includes bibliographical references and index.

Identifiers: LCCN 2019025138 | ISBN 9780870719714 (trade
    paperback)

Subjects: LCSH: Sports—Oregon—History. | Sports—Oregon—
    History—Pictorial works.

Classification: LCC GV584.O7 C36 2019 | DDC 796.09795—dc23

LC record available at https://lccn.loc.gov/2019025138

♾ This paper meets the requirements of ANSI/NISO Z39.48-1992
(Permanence of Paper).

Oregon State University
OSU Press

Oregon State University Press
121 The Valley Library
Corvallis OR 97331-4501
541-737-3166 • fax 541-737-3170
www.osupress.oregonstate.edu

OLSON, PORTLAND, P. C. L.

ORT, PORTLAND, P. C. L.

J. RYAN, PORTLAND, P. C. L.

D. RYAN, PORTLAND, P. C. L.

SPEAS, PORTLAND, P. C. L.

STEEN, PORTLAND, P. C. L.

CONTENTS

FOREWORD

Oregon was a very young state at the end of the 1860s—Oregon City was thirty years old, Portland was twenty-five, and the state itself was just completing its first decade with 91,000 people spread thinly over the landscape. Men outnumbered women by nearly three to two, a sign of the state's frontier resource economy. Only three cities counted more than 1,000 residents—Portland, Salem, and Oregon City. Fifty years later, when the last photographs in this collection were made, the state had grown up, with the 1920 census counting 788,000 Oregonians who lived a much more settled life than previous generations.

Competitive sports grew up with the state. The images that Brian Campf has assembled tell us about the growth of education, the establishment of a middle class, and the spread of railroads. They also testify to Oregonians' love of the outdoors.

If you wanted to play competitive team sports in nineteenth century Oregon, one of the big challenges was finding the competition. In the 1870s, Columbia River steamers plied the great river of the West; Willamette River steamboats connected river towns like Harrisburg, Salem, and Albany; and the first railroads connected Portland and East Portland to a string of Willamette Valley cities and towns. That was it for easy travel. Salem ballplayers could travel to Aurora with relative ease, or a McMinnville nine could take on a Portland team. Even in the 1910s, however, the only comfortable way to get from eastern Oregon to the western side of the state required changing trains in Portland. The images also remind us of the importance of Albany and Astoria in these decades. Albany rivaled Salem as the most important city in the upper Willamette Valley until Eugene nudged ahead in the early twentieth century, and Albany athletes make the third most appearances in this book. Astoria, which also appears repeatedly, ranked second only to Portland in the 1880s and 1890s.

Outside the northwestern quadrant of the state, competition was local. Campf documents separate constellations of competition in the Coos Bay area, in Umatilla County where at least nine towns had teams in the early 1910s and there was fierce competition among the members of the Blue Mountain League and the finely named but short-lived Irrigation League. The Inland Empire League stretched more ambitiously from Baker City (the Nuggets) to Walla Walla. Prineville, Bend, and Redmond put in their appearance in 1909, re-flecting the beginnings of central Oregon's timber industry and antic-ipating the resolution of the battle between James J. Hill of the Great Northern/Northern Pacific and E. H. Harriman of the Union Pacific/Southern Pacific to be the first to control the Deschutes River rail-road route.

Sports developed in step with the developing infrastructure of public education. Teams from the University of Oregon and Oregon Agricultural College garnered plenty of attention, tiny as the schools were compared to the institutions of the twenty-first century. Even more telling is the way that the images reflect the creation of com-prehensive public high schools as essential community institutions. Even though *Oregonian* editor Harvey Scott fulminated against pub-lic high schools as a waste of money (he fulminated against a lot of things), Portland established its first high school in 1869 in rented space, built a neo-gothic building in 1885, and then a modern Lincoln High School on the Park Blocks in 1912. Jefferson High School opened on the east side in 1908 and Gresham High School dates to 1906. And it was not only the larger cities, as we learn that Harney County High School had twelve seniors in 1911–1912, divided equally between boys and girls.

Campf concentrates on the big three teams sports—baseball and its community and semi-pro teams, football and its college teams, and basketball with its high school teams for boys and for girls who refused to play by wimpy "girls' rules." Oregonians, of course, had plenty of other ways to enjoy exercise and the outdoors. There were elite sports like rowing, lawn tennis, and golf (the Waverly Golf Club dates to 1896). English immigrants and ex-pats sporadically kept their ethnic sport of cricket alive in Portland. And there were out-door activities like fly-fishing where no one kept score (well, maybe the trout did). Energetic Portlanders joined the Mazamas, whose in-augural climb on July 19, 1894, took 158 men and 38 women to the top of Mt. Hood. If you didn't have time to summit a mountain, you could join the bicycle craze of the 1890s. Thousands of people took to the roads on Sunday cycling expeditions—sedate families, daredevil wheelmen, and "scorchers"—young men who rode too fast and too recklessly for most people's taste (what else is new). The *Road Book of Oregon*, published by the League of American Wheelmen in 1897, was free to members of the Oregon Division of the Wheelmen but a hefty $2.00 to others.

Oregon in the twenty-first century is embedded in a global economy. Its marquee professional teams respond to national markets, depend on instant communication, and draw on the global circulation of talent. In the nineteenth and early twentieth centuries, in contrast, Oregonians played each other, and occasionally teams from Washington. Team sports were community recreation and community endeavors, social "glue" and sources of community pride and frustration. On summer Sundays, I like to walk a few blocks to my local city park where there will usually be two or three softball games with bumbling amateur nines next to determined Latino nines playing serious baseball, all with friends and families, kids and dogs enjoying the afternoon. It's nice to think that Oregonians haven't changed that much in a hundred summers.

CARL ABBOTT
Portland State University, Emeritus

PREFACE

I have loved sports for as long as I can remember. I enjoy the anticipation of the game, watching the drama unfold, and seeing a winner and a loser. There is nothing else like it.

A few weeks shy of my tenth birthday I watched on television as the Portland Trail Blazers won the NBA title in 1977. My parents took us downtown for dinner that night. We found ourselves in the midst of a massive celebration. A picture of me near the podium at the Blazers championship parade the next day was published in *Hoop* magazine. My wife, Sandy, says that I remember the parade day as fondly as our wedding. I won't say if she's right.

Baseball was just as important to me. Portland had no major league team, but I followed the big leaguers and also Portland's minor league team, the Portland Beavers of the Pacific Coast League. When we were kids, my father, Alan, would take me and my brother, Andy, to their games at Portland's Civic Stadium. I began collecting baseball, basketball, and football cards around 1978, the same year as my first trip to the Memorial Coliseum to see the Blazers play.

NETZEL, PORTLAND, P. C. L.

A baseball card store opened in Portland in 1980. I insisted that my mother, Susan, drive me there. I must have been one of its earliest visitors. Though I was only about thirteen and had no money to spend, I loved my visit. Andy had come with us. A *Wall Street Journal* article published soon afterward described the store owner patiently answering the many questions from two unidentified youngsters (me and Andy).

Later in the 1980s, at the same store I stumbled across a baseball card. It showed a local player, a *Portland* player. The card was old and its history intrigued me. I snapped it up. This is the one: Miles Albion Netzel, issued in 1910 with Obak Cigarettes.

I thought it would be a fun challenge to seek out cards issued of other Portland players during that 1910 era and research their baseball careers. Around the same time I got to know several dealers of vintage baseball collectibles who helped me in that pursuit. They remain my friends to this day.

Then something changed everything: the arrival of the Internet. The Internet gave me access to Oregon sports objects, such as photos and postcards, that were dispersed across America. What had been far away suddenly became a few mouse clicks away from reaching my mailbox. I also began to look for items associated with Oregon sports other than baseball. With the Internet my collection expanded by leaps and bounds. I continued to enjoy investigating the history of each new piece. Sandy stopped asking about the little boxes that kept arriving.

The Internet also opened a door to new avenues of research. Keyword searches in century-old newspapers could be swiftly performed to reveal the stories behind a photo's charm and mystique. Period photography ultimately became a focus of the collection because it offers interesting and varied content, as well as locations and a more personal kind of connection to its subjects than objects such as trophies provide. Over the decades I acted like a magnet for these images, bringing them home to Oregon and into the archive, usually one at a time.

What emerged from my efforts is an archive of images I did not create but a collection I did create. I came to realize that anyone who says the fun is in the looking is seriously underestimating the satisfaction in the finding. It would be like saying the real fun of going on vacation is the plane ride. The pleasure for me came in adding something to the collection that gave it more depth and dimension.

I recall my mom asking me, "What are you going to do with all of this stuff?" I had no idea what to say so I answered, "Maybe a book one day." I had to say something, and in the back of my mind it seemed that if I said "book," there might actually be one. I also had begun to feel weird about squirreling this "stuff" away and being the only one who could see it. It is, after all, Oregon's history, and it deserves not just to be compiled, but preserved, seen, and enjoyed.

A website instead of a book seemed like a good place to start, sort of like learning to ride a bicycle before you drive a car. I store the entire collection in an enormous bank vault, so I started bringing home boxes of goodies from the bank, scanning it all, returning the boxes, and retrieving more, back and forth until the scanning was done. It was during one of those bank runs that someone nearly sideswiped my car. Were it not for some defensive driving that would have made my driving teacher proud, the contents of this book would look very different.

Seeing the website go live made me feel that I had conquered the law of gravity. I conceived of it as a free virtual museum. I researched each item and added brief descriptions I hoped would approximate placards on the wall next to objects hung in galleries. I also left my name off the site so it would be about "the" stuff and not "my" stuff, something that has necessarily and somewhat regrettably changed with the publication of this book.

The website (no longer active) showed Oregon sports material and also original images from my collection of early major league, minor league, and Negro league baseball. The site began receiving visitors who shared kind comments. The *Oregonian* even published a story about it. That encouragement helped push me toward making this book a reality. I liked the idea of a book offering a more permanent record than a website, plus it gave me the opportunity (read: awesome excuse) to research early Oregon sports.

After years of acquiring images and now sifting through them to decide what to include here, it occurs to me that if history is written by the victors, pictorial accounts are made possible by the collectors. I hope you enjoy this one.

INTRODUCTION

This introduction is like an arson investigation, which asks, How did the fire start? It addresses the origins and selection of images and provides context about the development of sports in Oregon. The rest of the book, the photo gallery, asks, What did the fire look like as it spread? To answer, I share selected images from the archive in mostly chronological order, accompanied by captions based on historical research for context. Team names, quotations, and citations in the book use spellings as they originally appeared, including the spelling of sports names (base ball, basket ball, foot ball).

THE PHOTOS

The first photograph in the gallery section, one of Oregon's earliest original sports photos, portrays Joseph Wiley in baseball attire in about 1867. He was a prominent Portland citizen who played for the city's first baseball team, the Pioneer Base Ball Club. The final images in the book are of the 1922 University of Oregon football program, followed by a baseball photograph that captures the appeal of competition. Between them are fifty-five years of a rich sports history.

These images reveal organized sports at their earliest. The athletic attire is antiquated. The equipment is old-fashioned. The small-town wooden ball parks are classic. Teams were being formed. Leagues were being created. Rivalries were brewing. To put those fifty-five years into perspective, the Cincinnati Reds became the first professional baseball team in 1869. In 1922, the American Professional Football Association changed its name to the National Football League.

Sporting Oregon contains primarily photos and postcards, with tickets and other ephemera mixed in. The volume of material that survived from before 1900 is much smaller than after 1900, when the postcards that form much of the collection were created. Postcards were likely saved for their messages, images on their fronts, and postmarks, all things that appeal to collectors. Those same factors—names on jerseys, period writing, postmarks and addresses—aid in identifying sports images.

Several types of photographs are included. Cartes de visite are photos mounted on a stiff backing about the size of a playing card. They typically date to the 1860s and 1870s. Cabinet photos are larger images mounted to a paper board and are usually from the 1880s through the early 1900s. Postcards with photos on their fronts—real photo postcards—became popular in the early 1900s. Tintypes, produced mostly in the second half of the nineteenth century, involved creating an image on iron (not tin, despite the name). The book includes one tintype.

Image quality—composition and clarity—informed the photo selections for *Sporting Oregon*. The quality of early pictures taken outside of a photo studio, especially by amateur photographers, varied widely. Photos with strong tones were favored for inclusion. Stacks of photos were excluded because they were too dark or too light.

Images with historical significance based on the person, place, or event shown were prioritized for inclusion. These are balanced by images that reflect the more everyday experiences of athletes. They are presented in roughly chronological order so that changing appearance and attire unfold and the image captions flow with the passage of time.

Research derived from period newspapers contributed heavily to the book's historical narrative and to the image captions. Presumably, those news articles accurately describe contemporaneous events, making them especially valuable. Quotes from articles are included to put the reader in the shoes of someone learning about matters as they occurred. Extensive sources cited in endnotes can assist in further study.

The photos generally reflect the overall geographical dispersion of the archive. The majority of images are from the Willamette Valley between Portland and Eugene. The remainder are from southern Oregon, eastern Oregon, and up and down the Oregon coast with a handful from less traveled areas.

Baseball, football, and basketball predominate because they constitute the majority of the archive, which attests to their popularity. Soccer, track, hockey, bowling, cricket, horse racing, auto racing, gymnastics, rowing, wrestling, and tennis all hold a worthy place in Oregon history and are also included. Collectively, these images portray men and women, amateurs and professionals, black and white, and young and old, all linked by a shared love of athletics.

No assemblage of photos can represent a full history of sports in a state, because the topic is vast, the surviving images reflect what someone chose to photograph, and the discretion used in amassing a collection means it is by definition incomplete. Instead, the images should be viewed as a compendium of pictures and stories once lost to time.

These sporting images transcend the score of any game, revealing human spirit and values. Their creation shows enthusiasm for athletics. Their preservation tugs at a nostalgia for earlier days. Fans cheering their teams display civic pride. The effort and expense of attending a sporting event imply a value placed on athletics. Modest attire and separated races reflect discarded social norms. Early equipment that now looks primitive is a reminder of its evolution. Vintage baseball cards show an admiration for athletes which continues unabated.

There are other inventories of early Oregon sports images in the hands of universities, historical societies, and private collectors. What sets *Sporting Oregon*'s collection apart is its lack of emphasis on one school or one sport. From baseball to basketball to football and more, it broadly represents the first fifty-five years of Oregon's athletic history.

THE RISE OF OREGON SPORTS

Baseball in Oregon began as a club sport. Football arose at a Portland educational academy. Basketball, invented at a Massachusetts YMCA, spread in part through that organization. The origin stories that follow start where the three main sports began in Oregon and end around the time they took hold. Nine key events stand out:

1. May 28, 1866: First meeting to form the Portland Pioneer Base Ball Club
2. October 13, 1866: First organized baseball "match game"
3. Circa 1888: Bishop Scott Academy organizes Oregon's first football team
4. November 27, 1890: First competitive football contest in Oregon
5. January 1893: Basketball is being played in Oregon by this time
6. November 3, 1893: First intercollegiate football game in Oregon
7. November 11, 1893: Oregon State University's first football game
8. March 24, 1894: University of Oregon's first football game
9. November 3, 1894: First Civil War football game

Jasper baseball team postcard, 1910.

BASEBALL

Baseball emerged nationally in the nineteenth century from related sports like town ball that shared its core features: striking a bat with a ball and moving between bases. Unlike basketball, invented in 1891, no singular moment gave rise to baseball. It formed gradually and moved from an amusement to a club sport to a professional one as it gained popularity.

The adoption of written rules by the New York Knickerbockers Base Ball Club on September 23, 1845—fourteen years before Oregon became a state, sixteen years before the Civil War began, and when baseball was spelled with two words—was a key moment in the game's evolution. Earlier teams had their own rules, but documentation did not survive the passage of time. The Knickerbockers' rules were written down, preserved, and formed the basis of how baseball is played today. They included reference to an umpire, team captains, bases, runs ("aces"), pitching, foul balls, outs, interference, a batting order, and the balk.

Baseball under those rules looked decidedly different from the game played today. The original rules omitted a fixed number of players per side required for a game. The first to twenty-one runs, with each side having an equal number of at-bats, was the winner. The distance from home to second and first to third was forty-two paces. Rules requiring nine players per side, nine innings, and ninety feet between bases—staples of modern baseball—arose in 1857 with the formation of baseball's first governing body, the National Association of Base Ball Players.

In 1869, the Cincinnati Red Stockings became the first professional team of paid players. They finished the season undefeated at 57–0. The inaugural professional league, the National Association of Professional Base Ball Players, was created in 1871. The National League began in 1876, and the first minor league, the Northwestern

League, started in 1879. At the other end of the spectrum was amateur baseball. As baseball grew in popularity, so did the number of local clubs whose rosters were filled by athletes playing for the love of the game.

It was against that backdrop that the first pitch for organized baseball in Portland was thrown. Nine of the city's young athletes gathered in the office of J. W. Cook, a bag factory, on the evening of Monday, May 28, 1866, to form a team.[1] Three of the nine were assigned to a committee on invitations for club membership. Three others were tasked with drafting a constitution. One of them was to negotiate for a place to play.

They met again on June 2 and emerged with team officers and a name befitting them: the Pioneer Base Ball Club (PBBC). Thirty members were added to the club's rolls just over two weeks later, including Joseph Buchtel, a player who managed the club and would become the face of early Portland baseball. Thirty-one men from among the city's population of 6,508 signed a constitution the club adopted. Portland was a small town then, with one architect, four hardware stores, six restaurants, nine bakeries, and one astrologer.[2]

Bat and ball games were not new to Oregon. One of baseball's predecessor games, town ball, had been played in Oregon since the pioneer days. In a 1900 *Oregonian* story, an Oregonian born in 1848 recalled his experience with the sport as a boy: "One of the principal games we played was town ball, which answers to our baseball of today, though played very differently." In selecting teams, first pick was decided using the "ball bat." It was three to six inches wide at the top and whittled down to a handhold. The best player on one team would spit on one side of the bat, toss it with a twirl in the air while asking "wet or dry," and the opposing lead player called out one or the other. The side of the bat facing up determined first pick.

Which team batted first was sometimes settled by the leader of one team tossing the bat to his counterpart, who would hold it near the middle. They would alternate handholds up to the top of the bat. The team of the player with the last handhold strong enough to toss the bat over his head would bat first. As for playing town ball,

> The ballground had four corners, similar to our baseball ground, with a pitcher and a catcher. We did not know anything about curves, but threw the ball over-hand right from the shoulder. We did not stand on the bases as in the modern game. The striker [batter] had to run the bases, and if we could catch the ball on the fly or on the first bound the striker was out. If, when he ran from one base to the next, we could throw the ball in front of him, that is, between him and the base he was

trying to reach, he was out. If we could hit him with the ball while he was running from one base to the next, he was out. It would be surprising how quickly one side could be caught out and the other side let in.

Balls for town ball were made by unraveling an old sock or stocking and wrapping the yarn around a piece of leather until it was the right size. Then "we would carry in the wood and do all kinds of chores to get mother to cover it with a piece of old pants leg or coat sleeve." Other games they played included base, and for smaller boys, a bat and ball game called three-cornered cat.[3]

A Medford resident claimed to have organized Oregon's first baseball team in Corvallis in 1856, ten years before the Pioneers formed. "No, it wasn't 'town ball' we played, but the original game of baseball," he told the *Medford Mail Tribune* in 1910. Their only equipment was a bat whittled from native wood and a ball that at first was rubber and later was made of yarn covered in buckskin with a rubber center. "That ball was the most valuable piece of property belonging to the club," he added. "If in playing in open fields, as we did in those days, the ball was 'lost,' the game was called until the players, spectators and even the umpire had searched until they found it."[4]

In 1922, the *Oregonian* printed, "The Pioneer baseball club is really supposed to be the first team the city ever had, although there were several small-fry teams playing about the same time and later."[5] Given the account of the Medford resident, anecdotes of earlier bat and ball games, and baseball's popularity elsewhere, it is far-fetched to believe that nobody in Oregon played baseball before the Pioneers. Those contests, though, would have been informal and intermittent, while the Pioneers played within the structure of a club organized for its members around baseball.

The Pioneers elected officers, adopted a constitution, and had business meetings. They held practices, arranged games, and had designated baseball grounds in Oregon's largest city. They wore team uniforms and encouraged fan attendance. Indeed, in October 1866, Pioneer team president Theodore Miner called Oregon's second club to form, Clackamas, "second in the field, by date of organization," meaning the Pioneers were first. That same month, the New York–based periodical *New York Clipper* called the Pioneer club "the first formed in the State." In 1867, the club described itself as "the pioneer Base Ball Club of Oregon."[6]

With no other local clubs to compete against, the Pioneers assembled teams to play from within their own ranks. The local press was behind them from the start. Less than two months after the team formed, the *Oregonian* called baseball "exhilarating," observed that the spirit of the Pioneer's play showed that "its enlivening effects are by no means a small matter," and called the club's progress "remarkable."[7]

In 1866, the Pioneers initially played in downtown Portland on "grounds" (an early term for a baseball field) west of the Oregon Iron Works on the corner of Morrison and Seventh, and then on another field on Oak Street between Fifth and Sixth. They also used east side grounds located "a few rods south of the Stark street ferry landing." (A rod measures 16.5 feet.) This was before bridges were built across the Willamette River in Portland. "The new ferry boat will leave the foot of Stark street every ten minutes" for the east side, the *Oregonian* advised before an August 1866 match.[8]

The Pioneers wore a baseball shirt affixed with a shield bearing the PBBC team insignia over their regular clothes. A description of what they wore in 1873, though seven years later, gives a sense of the sport's attire of that era: "At the last meeting of the Pioneer Club the Committee on Uniform reported that they had decided on obtaining blue pants, white shirts with blue cuffs and collars with red breast place [*sic*] in which the letter "P" would be set, cut out of blue," and finished off with a black cap and belt.[9]

The baseballs had a large rubber core wrapped with twine and covered with horsehide. "In those days the live balls would bounce and catching a ball on the first bounce was the same as catching a fly. It put the man out," Buchtel explained. They wore no gloves, and "when a hot liner came it was a case of grabbing it no matter how live a ball it was."[10]

Scores then were far higher than today. The 1860s were not the days of one-hundred-mile-per-hour fastballs. Batters could specify where they wanted the balls pitched, such as between the knees and shoulder. The pitcher gave an underhand toss of the ball (the overhand throw was not commonly used until 1876). The distance between the pitcher and batter, then called a striker, was just forty-five feet (in the National League that distance went to fifty feet in 1881, and in 1893 it was extended to the sixty feet, six inches still used today.)[11]

The Pioneer's first test came on a cool, cloudy, windless August day at the Oak Street grounds. The club chose two teams from among its members to play for what they called a "championship." "Lady visitors" were given on-field seats. The game was a hit, and the *Oregonian* gave it a high score. The batting: "excellent." The defense: strong despite "the irregularity of the field." The teams: "pretty evenly chosen" by the team captains, a judgment seen in the box score showing the final tally: 28–24. The attendance: "tolerably fair." Some disappointed spectators had arrived at the end of the game, perhaps because an advertisement in the *Oregonian* gave a 4 p.m. start while a news report listed it at 4:30 p.m. [12]

The Dickson Baseball Dictionary defines what the Pioneers had played as a "friendly match," one between members of the same club as opposed to a match game "played between two organized clubs that resulted from a formal challenge and was played for a specific stake (usually a new ball), often on a best two-of-three basis." The *Oregonian* called this August contest and others involving only Pioneer club members a "match game."[13] Technically, match game was the wrong term, but it correctly implied the sides played to win.

"The ball fever has 'broken out in a new place,' and the denizens of far distant Oregon, the northwestern extremity of Uncle Samuel's dominions, are now infected with the complaint in an alarming degree," reported the *New York Clipper*, which covered baseball extensively. "They played a practice game—the first, it is said, which ever came off in Oregon—on August 3d, with the appended result: Fielding nine, 24; Batting nine, 28." In baseball's vernacular of that time a practice game was, per *The Dickson Baseball Dictionary*, "an exhibition game, as opposed to a match game."[14]

Team meetings, practices, and game reports appeared in the *Oregonian*. For an August 1866 contest in East Portland, the newspaper had been asked to note that "ladies are especially invited to witness the game." Perhaps the Pioneers desired to meet them, or they hoped women fans or their male counterparts would increase attendance, or both. That contest resulted in "a few days confinement" for Joseph Buchtel of the Pioneers. He had sprained his right ankle while making the game's only home run. The team's starters, known as the first nine, were selected, and Buchtel organized a second team from the club to practice with them." First nine meant "the nine players who, when available, represented a baseball club in a match game." The second nine was "a team in an early baseball club made up of players not quite good enough for the *first nine*. Members of the second nine would fill in for absent members of the first nine, but second nines also often issued their own challenges to either the first nine or second nine of another club."[15]

"This athletic sport is now the rage throughout the whole country, and our city is not behind," the *Oregonian* proclaimed. The problem was that the Pioneers had no one else to play, but that was not the case for long. The *Oregonian* revealed on September 24, 1866, that the Clackamas Base Ball Club had formed and was playing regularly.

Based in Oregon City, its games to that point, like the Pioneers, were restricted to members of its own club.[16]

Following baseball courtesies of the day, the Clackamas club "challenged" the Pioneers to a Saturday, October 13, game in Oregon City, one Portland promptly accepted at a special club meeting. Two words in the *Oregonian*—"A Challenge"—signified the start of competitive baseball in Oregon. That newspaper printed an advance list of the Clackamas players and a trip itinerary. The Pioneers played a practice game, and the paper assured readers that "the boys are all doing their best for the match game to be played at Oregon City on Saturday next."[17]

On game day for Oregon's first baseball contest between organized clubs, the Pioneers and "a number of ladies from this city" left Portland at 6 a.m. on the steamer *Senator* bound for Oregon City. There they were met with fanfare by the first nine of the Clackamas team and the Oregon City brass band. They ate together at the Barlow House where "the party did ample justice to a splendid breakfast," and then went to the ball grounds about a mile from the city for the game. The only reported glitch that day was in how the field was arranged: "A mistake was made in laying out the ground, the pitcher, basemen, and fielders, all were stationed facing the sun. This was unfortunate, as the playing was made unpleasant by this disposition of the men." The teams played on, and the Pioneers prevailed 77–45 in two hours and forty minutes. Hall of Famer Henry Chadwick, a sportswriter and baseball advocate who invented the modern box score, kept a newspaper account of the match (it included a box score) in his scrapbook.[18]

"This is the first match game ever played in the State and it is a splendid beginning," the *Oregonian* cheered. After the game, Clackamas offered the Pioneers the ball, "which was very properly refused, as the game was a friendly one and not for blood." In fact, it *was* a match game played in response to a challenge, but there was no prize at stake.

Toasts, speeches, and champagne flowed at a post-game dinner at the Barlow House. Referencing baseball players who had stopped playing to fight in the Civil War, which had ended just fourteen months earlier, Pioneer center fielder James Steel toasted "America's sons of the Base Ball fraternity, who for four years dropped the *bat* and *ball* to carry the *musket* and *ball* until they made the rebels bawl for quarter." On the lighter side, Steel offered a pun on the name of Clackamas pitcher S. D. Pope: "Why are the members of the Clackamas Base Ball Club like the people of Rome? Because they have a Pope among them."[19]

The Pioneers gained legitimacy by joining the National Association of Base Ball Players, the governing body charged with enacting the rules of play for its members. At its New York City convention on December 12, 1866, the association appointed the Pioneer's delegate, Robert H. Law, to its printing committee, enhancing the club's status. The Pioneers delayed opening their 1867 season until Law's return (he had been in New York for the previous six months) because they anticipated he would bring with him "the latest established rules."[20]

In November 1866, the *Oregonian* stated, "We expect that next season will see the establishment of many new clubs, and that Oregon will not be behindhand in representing the national game." In March 1867, the newspaper added:

> It has also been suggested that another club be formed. There are, certainly, a great number of young men in this city who could well enough afford the time and the trifling expense of supporting another club. The friendly rivalry which would naturally spring up between two such clubs would be a great promoter of the zeal and progress of each. We hope to see the Pioneers take the field, and in common with many others, also, hope to see a rival club organized. [21]

Portland responded, with April 1867 bringing news that a new club would soon appear. It was most likely the Wide Awake Base Ball Club, which organized in May and named Samuel Buchtel, Joseph Buchtel's brother, as the team captain. However, it was not the third team in Oregon behind the Pioneers and Clackamas: Roseburg had by then formed a club and was holding weekly "meetings" (probably referring to practices).[22]

The ball kept rolling. Portland had at least six clubs by July 31. Perhaps one was short a player when a brewery's wagon driver "stopped last evening on the base-ball grounds and engaged in the game there going on." He hit the ball, ran, fell, and broke his left arm near the elbow. The *Oregonian's* report of the accident added, "We understand that Drs. Glisan and Wilson will make the attempt this morning to adjust the fractures."[23]

A proposal to form a state baseball organization for the purpose of playing an undetermined California team for the state championship was endorsed by the *Oregon City Enterprise* in March 1867—"Good idea," it editorialized.[24] Research has found no record of such a game, but the very idea highlights the growing momentum behind baseball in Oregon.

Baseball fever also struck Salem. In November 1866, the *Oregon City Enterprise* anticipated that the next year Salem would field a team. Things went as expected. March 30: "A club will be formed at Salem." May 29: "A base ball club has been organized at Salem." June 19: "We have two organized clubs [in Salem], and three others talked of. We understand it is the intention of some or all of these clubs to enter the list for the championship at the approaching State Fair." July 22: "This city now supports seven churches, nine saloons and beer shops, two lodges of Good Templars, and eight base ball clubs!"[25]

After defeating Clackamas in the game on October 13, 1866, the Pioneers beat them again in June 1867 on a sultry afternoon in Portland, 78–36, and in July in Oregon City by a 55–44 score in a game "contested with ardor by all engaged." The wins gave the Pioneers the right to call themselves state champions, a status they would defend at the state fair. Per a September 1867 report in the *Oregonian*, "This morning appears a notice from the Pioneer Base Ball Club, that the first nine will play, if challenged, at the coming State Fair, any club in Oregon or Washington Territory. Here is a chance to win or lose laurels. Who speaks first?"[26]

The Clackamas club did, but misspoke. A chastisement in the newspaper quickly appeared and explained their violation of baseball protocol: "We notice by the [*Oregon City*] *Enterprise* that the Clackamas club has accepted the challenge of the Pioneers to play a match at the State Fair. The Pioneers have not issued any challenge; but merely signified their readiness to *accept* a challenge from any other club. Being thus far, the champion club, according to the courtesy of the game, they receive, but do not issue, challenges."[27]

Ultimately, the Pioneers accepted challenges from Salem's Willamette team and the Clackamas club. On October 9, two days after dispatching the Willamettes 92–25 in just short of three hours, the Pioneer club captured state fair baseball honors with a 58–53 win over Clackamas, and with it a $40 ball and bat prize. "The 'crowd' caught the spirit of the game, and often waved hats and handkerchiefs and cheered."[28]

Given the local enthusiasm for baseball, it was only a matter of time before it was used as a marketing tool. The month after their Oregon State Fair win, an advertisement for Christmas toys at Portland's McCormick's Book Store abbreviated baseball as "B. B." and rhymed, "I've *Furniture, Fiddles,* and *French Fusileers* [*sic*], *Soldiers* that look like B. B. Pioneers."[29]

Joseph Buchtel was a photographer by trade and he displayed in his galleries trophies the Pioneers had collected. They included the bat prize won at the 1867 state fair. It was made of four different kinds of wood—white and black walnut, Oregon maple, and mahogany—and had inscribed engravings on two silver plates. Winning the bat took less time than receiving it. At a June 1868 team business meeting, the Pioneers instructed their secretary to ask about the prize: "The club wants to know when the bat is to be handed over."[30]

The Pioneers looked good at the state fair in both play and attire. In August 1867, a steamer delivered a dozen baseball caps manufactured to order in San Francisco. The *Oregonian* described the uniforms: "The caps are decidedly gay in appearance, the body being bright scarlet, with a visor, white on the upper side and green beneath. On the top of the crown is a silver-colored star. The caps are very light and comfortable."[31]

Who was playing on these clubs? On Portland's Pioneers it was "young men of this city who are fond of athletic sports." More teams meant more players and that meant people from all walks of life played the game. The *Oregonian's* traveling correspondent sent a dispatch from Salem describing the scene there in July 1867:

> It's funny to see my old friends—well, I'll not mention them—playing *base ball. Old* fellows and young fellows, tall and short fellows, rich and poor, State officers and citizens, all play, and if sprained ankles, crippled fingers, and battered shins are marks of good players, why, the Salem boys are experts.
>
> Well, base ball makes lots of fun for the town people, but the hard working country folk, who have plenty of useful exercise, growl about having to pay for newspapers filled up with base ball nonsense.

"It is spoken of as 'The game' as though it were the only game known," the *Oregonian* noted in the same issue.[32] By the end of 1867, at least twenty-nine teams from eight Oregon cities had taken the field, though how long they lasted is unknown (see the appendix). They include the Pioneer, Wide Awake, and Spartan clubs of Portland; the Clackamas, Highland, and Tumwater clubs of Oregon City; the Pacific, Willamette, and Union clubs of Salem; and the Dysodia club of Eugene.

Baseball's rise in Eugene was typical of the time. In June 1867, between an article on a new sidewalk leading to a stable and one on a law office opening opposite a saddle shop: "Base Ball—Why not have a base ball club in Eugene? There is not a town on the river below here but what has an organized club." Three weeks later: "The 'Dysodia Base Ball Club' is the name of our society for the development of the muscles." Four weeks after that: "An exciting match game of Base Ball between the married and single men of this city occurred last Wednesday afternoon."[33]

Even in those first days of Oregon baseball the game evoked patriotism. The *Oregon City Enterprise* told readers that before the Clackamas club's 1867 Independence Day match against the Pioneers, a 150-foot "liberty pole" would be raised on the team's grounds, "from which 'the glorious old banner' will be flung to the breeze."[34]

The talents of teams varied, and that led to some 1860s trash talk. After Salem's Willamettes lost 92–25 to the Pioneers, the *Oregonian* asked, "Wonder if there is not some *easier* game at which the Willamettes could play—say, pins, or marbles!" Albany's *State Rights Democrat* sought to preempt criticism of its city's new team by warning in June 1868 that they were "a little awkward" in their game, and squabbled over fair and foul balls and base running. But, the newspaper advised, "The playing of the 'Web-foot Base Ball Club' will soon be brought down to a science, and then the 'Pioneers' at Portland, and 'them other fellers' up and down the river must look out for their laurels, because we expect to 'go for em.'"[35]

The Pioneers indeed should have looked out for their laurels because they were seized two months later, but not by the Albany club. Under the heading "Lost Once," the *Oregonian* reported on having been informed that the Pioneers' 123–76 loss to the Clackamas club on August 22, 1868, in Oregon City was their first-ever defeat.[36]

While teams were composed of amateurs and games were played as a gentlemanly club sport, the players still wanted to win, and that required practice. Pioneer players found a stern warning about being tardy for practice in the July 1, 1867, *Oregonian*: "The President of the Pioneer Base Ball Club requests us to say to the members that punctuality is absolutely essential when called upon to practice. Be on the ground at the minute announced in the call, and others will not have lost time (nor patience) in being as all should be—punctual."[37]

The Pioneers did not suffer this problem alone. The July 2 *Oregonian* repeated the message, but with the Portland team Wide Awake substituted for Pioneer.[38] Promptness by players was apparently not a new concern nor one unique to Portland teams. The 1845 rules of the New York Knickerbocker Base Ball Club began: "Members must strictly observe the time agreed upon for exercise, and be punctual in their attendance."

Players sought to develop winning strategies. The *Oregonian* remarked favorably in June 1867 about Clackamas pitcher S. D. Pope's technique of pitching the ball with a very slight momentum and causing it to form a "beautiful curve" so it was on a downward incline when it reached the batter. This was not the modern curve ball. "We didn't have any curves in those days. The only way we could fool a batter was to pretend to give him a swift ball and then let it come slow," Joseph Buchtel explained in the *Oregon Daily Journal*, describing a pitch that today is called the change-up. A pitching innovator, Buchtel developed an underhand throw that would send the ball directly behind him or to one side without changing position, perfect for picking off a runner. "After using the throw for a while effectively

City View Park near what is now Sellwood Park; the Clinton & McCoy ground along the riverbank in southeast Portland south of what was then Stephens Slough (in the vicinity of SE Division Street); and the West End ball grounds south of City Park, now Washington Park, where the grandstand could accommodate twelve hundred people.[55]

Notable baseball figures have played on Portland's grounds. The first black player in organized baseball in the twentieth century—and also the first one to appear on an American baseball card—was Jimmy Claxton, who had pitched for an African American team in Portland in 1914 and 1915.[56] Playing for Portland's professional teams were the Olympian Jim Thorpe, and Hall of Famers Dave Bancroft, Mickey Cochrane, Stan Coveleski, Harry Heilmann, Billy Southworth, Joe Tinker, Heine Manush, and Satchel Paige (the last two very briefly Portland players). Oregonians Joe Gordon and Bobby Doerr are also members of baseball's Hall of Fame.

The Pioneers remain the common ancestor of all Oregon baseball clubs. They live on through teams that play today and also through clubs that now compete using period rules and attire under names including Pioneers and Willamettes. They laid the foundation for baseball as Oregon's oldest major sport and set the stage for it to thrive throughout the state.

Ex-Oregon Agricultural College athlete and assistant
football coach Everett May, circa 1914.

FOOTBALL

The date was November 27, 1890. Something new to Oregon was unfolding in northwest Portland on that Thanksgiving Day: separately organized teams playing a football game—not rugby, not soccer, but *football*. Fifteen hundred of Portland's 85,000 residents had gathered at the Bishop Scott Academy on NW Nineteenth and Couch for the contest.[1]

Far from Oregon, gridiron football (so called for its field markings) had been emerging as a collegiate sport. Rutgers and Princeton played the first intercollegiate football game on November 6, 1869, though under rules very different than today's. By 1890, Rutgers, Princeton, Harvard, Yale, and Dartmouth were among the schools that fielded football teams.

America was maturing as a nation during that period. Ratification of the Fifteenth Amendment giving black men the right to vote was three months away when that first college game was played. When fans gathered in 1890 for the football game at Bishop Scott, North Dakota, South Dakota, Montana, and Washington had been states for just a year.

Football rules were developing, as well. At the time of the 1890 contest, the rules called for eleven players per side, a line of scrimmage, three downs to go five yards to retain possession, and Rule 17: "No one wearing projecting nails or iron plates on his shoes, or any metal substance upon his person, shall be allowed to play in a match."[2] The forward pass was illegal until 1906, making football in those prior decades a game of muscle and might.

On one side of the ball in white canvas uniforms and navy blue stockings was the team from Bishop Scott, a Portland military school. Leading them was John Gavin, who began organized football in Oregon by starting a team there after joining its faculty. "He is a Yale man, and, although he did not belong to the college eleven, was always prominent in football circles," the *Oregonian* explained. Another *Oregonian* article recalled the team:

> The installation of football, played under college rules, in the Northwest, was by a coterie of Eastern college men and football enthusiasts, who constituted the faculty of the Bishop Scott academy, of this city. Among the faculty were football players of more or less experience who had gained their football knowledge in Eastern or English universities.
>
> A football club was organized, helped out by several husky Western cadets, and, under the coaching of Professor J. W. Gavin, a code of signals was adopted and daily practice was begun.

The exact year when the team formed is uncertain. A former Bishop Scott player thought Gavin came to the academy near 1886 and introduced football around a year later, but a report on education in Portland states he joined Bishop Scott in 1887. One *Oregonian* article reports he started there in 1888 and soon after Bishop Scott had three football teams, while another claims he organized the football team in 1889.[3] He first appears in the *Portland City Directory* in 1889, so his arrival was likely the year before.

Across the ball from Bishop Scott that day was the Portland Amateur Athletic Club (PAAC) team. The PAAC had organized in August 1890 under a different name, the Portland Football, Cricket and Athletic Association. Before 1890, "football" in Oregon meant

1887 Bishop Scott Academy envelope, around the time football began to be played there.

have been five to a team. The rules have been standardized of late years, and basketball, in its improved form, promises to become the great American indoor sport."[18] Indeed it did, and it remains so today.

Oregon trade card with fishing motif, 1889.

OTHER SPORTS

The origins of other sports in Oregon are difficult to discern. Legions grew up with the Portland Buckaroos and Winter Hawks hockey teams, winners of multiple titles. The Portland Timbers won a 2015 championship and affirmed the city's love for soccer. Runner Steve Prefontaine called the world's attention to track in Oregon at the 1972 Olympics. Yet no singular moment gave rise to those sports locally. Frozen ponds long ago gave way to hockey, open fields to soccer, and there has been track for as long as athletes have run and jumped.

What is clear is that if there was a sport, Oregonians played it. In the winter of 1805 and 1806, the Lewis and Clark Expedition camped at Fort Clatsop along the Clatsop Plains. Ninety-one winters later, skaters traveled by train from Astoria to those frozen plains to play ice hockey and other sports. In 1916, the Portland Rosebuds became the first US hockey team to play for the Stanley Cup, losing to the Montreal Canadiens.[1]

The Portland Cricket Club lost at home to the Victoria Cricket Club in 1878, but "Prof. Brenner's fine band played throughout the match, and Mr. J. Reed successfully catered for the wants of the inner man." A best-of-five lacrosse series was held for "the championship at Portland" in September 1885. The Portland Polo Club and the Eugene Amateur Polo Club were to square off for the state title in 1886 in Eugene, admission twenty-five cents with a "social hop" to follow. In 1896, a Portland resident was in Gearhart putting in a set of golf links. [2]

On the national scene, Portland has hosted golf's Ryder Cup, the women's world amateur softball championship, the final four college basketball tournament, and Davis Cup tennis. In softball, a tip of the cap goes to the women of Portland's Amateur Softball Association national champion teams, the Lind and Pomeroy Florists (1944) and Erv Lind Florists (1964). Michael Jordan, Larry Bird, and Magic Johnson—and Portland's own Clyde Drexler—brought unsurpassed basketball talent to the city in 1992 for Olympic qualifying games. Nike, headquartered near Beaverton, Oregon, has outfitted athletes around the world.[3]

Finally, though it is not a conventional sport, the opportunity to recount the *Oregonian's* enthusiasm in 1866 upon receiving something called an "elastic gymnastic return ball" cannot be missed: "Adults, as well as children, are prone to try their skill with the new invention, which consists of a round red ball, attached to an elastic cord, and fastened to the finger by a ring, and when thrown from the hand returns to the same, by means of the cord, and the skill of the player is exercised in throwing and catching it thirty times in a minute."

PHOTO GALLERY

Portland Pioneer Base Ball Club player Joseph Wiley (1844–1894) stares intently into the camera in a circa 1867 carte de visite, a photo mounted on a stiff board. He served as school superintendent of Multnomah County, a Portland police force captain, a captain in the military organization Emmet Guard, a Portland city councilor, the proprietor and editor of the *Catholic Sentinel*, and volunteer fireman. Photo studios around Oregon were relatively few in number then—there were more baseball clubs in the state than photographers by the end of 1867—making sports images from that period very scarce. [1]

Portland Pioneer Base Ball Club members Joseph Buchtel (top), Joseph Wiley (bottom left), and an unknown player wearing a jersey that on close inspection reads "PBBC" pose on this carte de visite that bears a handwritten date of November 25, 1870. Buchtel (1830–1916), an acquaintance of President Lincoln, came to Oregon as a pioneer in 1852. He had traveled overland with a party that had sixty ox teams. "Mr. Buchtel proceeded from The Dalles by sailboat and canoe down the Columbia to the Cascades, and thence crossed the Cascade Mountains to Portland," the *Oregonian* recounted. He opened photo galleries in Portland, Astoria, and Oregon City, helped to organize Portland's volunteer fire department and became its chief, was sheriff of Multnomah County, invented fire equipment, and was an organizer of the Pioneer Base Ball Club, for which he was captain, manager, and pitcher. [2]

This circa 1870 tintype (a photo on iron, not tin), reportedly from an album of early photos that included images by Portland photographer Joseph Buchtel, a leading member of the city's Pioneer Base Ball Club, likely depicts Oregon baseball players.

Albany's A. B. Paxton photographed a jockey casually leaning against a chair in this carte de visite from circa 1875. "A. B. Paxton, Albany's popular photographer, is daily winning new laurels in his beautiful art,"[3] the Albany *State Rights Democrat* lauded in 1873. The image is hand-colored to depict a blue hat with a red stripe, a blue vest with red sleeves and red buttons, white pants, and yellow stockings. The reverse provides, "Negatives preserved. Additional copies 25 cents. Positively not printed, unless paid for when ordered."

An 1884 billhead for Portland's William Beck & Son's Sportsmen's Emporium, established in 1852, promoted baseball goods, croquet, birdcages, roller skates, and more. One of their advertisements appeared in the *Eugene City Guard* in 1884 on the same page as ads offering remedies for tuberculosis (then called consumption), pain (Dr. Smith's Caloric Vita Oil, the "Best Pain Killer and Healing Remedy in the World"), and erectile dysfunction (an "electric belt" with this pledge: "There is no mistake about this instrument, the continuous stream of ELECTRICITY permeating through the parts must restore them to healthy action.")[4]

Opposite: Astoria hosted a firemen's tournament in June 1885. An African American stands at the front of the Salem No. 3 team in the twelve-man hose race. It is unknown if the image depicts the dry contest (run three hundred yards to a hydrant, attach the hose, lay three hundred feet of hose, screw on the nozzle, and let it touch the ground) or the wet contest (run two hundred yards to a hydrant, attach the hose, lay three hundred feet of hose, and get water). The Salem No. 3 entry lost both races, each of which paid $150 for first place. The other photo shows the start of the three hundred yard footrace, which paid a $50 top prize. [5]

Partridge   Opposite the Post Office, PORTLAND, OR.

Partridge   Firemen in 330 Yard Foot Race.   No. 3902.   Opposite the Post Office, PORTLAND, OR.
                   Firemen's Tournament at Astoria, June 1885.

43

Photographer Samuel Graham took this image of nine men posing with a sleeping dog around 1886–1887, when he had an East Portland gallery.[6] Though they do not look like a sporting nine, the number needed for baseball, the person seated in the front, third from the left, appears to hold a ball, the two standing individuals grasp a bat, and the player standing on the left wears what looks like a baseball uniform.

Portland's Imperial Studio captured this cabinet photo of a jockey clutching a riding crop in both hands while standing on studio "grass" in about 1889.

The date of this McMinnville team photo is unclear, though many of the players shown played for McMinnville in 1890 and another copy of the photo that has surfaced bears an 1890 date. A note on this photo states, "The best base ball team that ever played in Yamhill Co. Never defeated," but an 1890 news article refers to a McMinnville loss. Perhaps the note accompanying the image was written prior to the defeat. Fan enthusiasm at two 1890 games between McMinnville and Salem left Salem's *Evening Capital Journal* griping, "There is too much hollowing [*sic*: hollering] from those in the grand stand."[7]

Advertising for M. T. Nolan, a dealer in "Books, Stationery and Varieties" in The Dalles, was printed on this comic baseball trade card. The card probably dates to the early 1890s, as by 1891 advertisements for Nolan's "The Postoffice Store" appeared in the press. It may have belonged to a student because the reverse bears a handwritten list of oceans: Arctic, Atlantic, Pacific, Indian, and Antarctic. Someone has colored parts of the image in purple. As for the caption, a baseball dictionary defines "daisy cutter" as "a sharply hit ground ball along the surface of the ground without rebounding, presumably removing any daisies in its path."[8]

Four Portland Rowing Club members wearing sport PRC jerseys, photographed in 1891 by Elbridge Moore. The club was formed that year after an 1890 flood had swept away most of the belongings of its predecessor, the Portland Rowing Association.[9] An advertising card for Moore's photography business from the same time period warns on the reverse, "Scores of people will come in and say, 'well we have been taken in by the cheap photographer, and now we want some photos made where we know we will be satisfied at a fair price.'"

A circa 1892 envelope touted "Base Ball Goods, Croquet, Baby Carriages, etc., etc." at Cohen, Davis & Co., located on First Street in Portland. An ad for Portland's International Hotel is at its top left. The front of an advertising card for that hotel, located on Third and E (now Everett) in northwest Portland, suggests how that block looked then. The hotel's pledge on the card and on the envelope, "No Chinese Employed," reveals the social acceptance of that appalling sentiment, one reflected in the national Chinese Exclusion Act that was enacted in 1882 and not repealed until 1943.

These circa 1892 athletes, each one on the right missing their right leg, embody true courage. The taller baseball player leans on a bat for the photo taken by an Independence studio. The other photograph, taken in Monmouth, shows a pair of gymnasts.

The Willamette River has long made Portland a natural spot for the sport of rowing. Portland's Willamette Rowing Club issued this invitation in 1893: "The Willamette Rowing Club will hold the first of its regular monthly housewarmings tonight. An excellent musical and literary programme will be rendered, and a pleasant time is expected. Nearly 250 invitations have been issued. The boathouse will be appropriately decorated for the occasion," the *Oregonian* announced. The function was well attended and also included brief speeches and a club swinging athletic exhibition.[10]

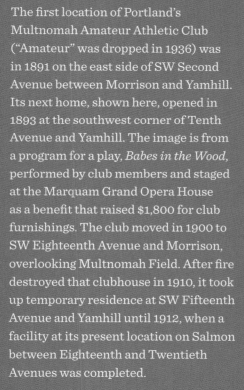

The first location of Portland's Multnomah Amateur Athletic Club ("Amateur" was dropped in 1936) was in 1891 on the east side of SW Second Avenue between Morrison and Yamhill. Its next home, shown here, opened in 1893 at the southwest corner of Tenth Avenue and Yamhill. The image is from a program for a play, *Babes in the Wood,* performed by club members and staged at the Marquam Grand Opera House as a benefit that raised $1,800 for club furnishings. The club moved in 1900 to SW Eighteenth Avenue and Morrison, overlooking Multnomah Field. After fire destroyed that clubhouse in 1910, it took up temporary residence at SW Fifteenth Avenue and Yamhill until 1912, when a facility at its present location on Salmon between Eighteenth and Twentieth Avenues was completed.

Will Lipman dances at the far left of a page excerpted from a program for *Babes in the Wood,* a play the men of the Multnomah Amateur Athletic Club performed in 1893 to raise money for clubhouse furnishings. He coached the Portland Amateur Athletic Club in Oregon's first game of American football between separately organized teams. The contest was played against Bishop Scott Academy in 1890. Lipman and other members of the PAAC broke away and formed the Multnomah Club in 1891 after a dispute arose within their former club.

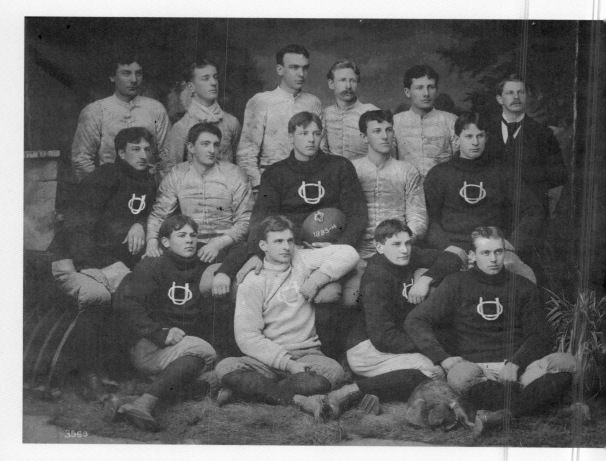

"The University of Oregon at Eugene is to have a foot ball team," the *Albany Daily Democrat* announced on March 1, 1894. Less than three weeks later, Eugene's Winter Photo Company captured this image, as duly noted in the *Daily Eugene Guard*: "The university foot ball team had a group photograph taken this afternoon." They trounced Albany College 44–2 on March 24 in Eugene to win the only game they played that season. "The home team must pay the expenses of the visitors, hence an admittance fee will be charged. Those who desire to witness the game next Saturday can procure tickets at either of the bookstores and Henderson & Linn's drug store. Price 25 cents," the *Eugene City Guard* advised.[12] Now called the Ducks, the University of Oregon's teams were long called the Webfooters or Webfoots.

The first Civil War contest was not a football game, but rather a baseball game played nearly six months before the schools met on the gridiron. The University of Oregon ball club visited Corvallis in 1894 and defeated Oregon Agricultural College 32–23, according to a story in *The Dalles Daily Chronicle*, which reported a favorable impression of the visitors, seen in this 1893–1894 team photo: "We can say of the Eugene boys that during our attendance at the State Agricultural College we have never met a better set of young athletic gentlemen. Although this is the first time they visited the OAC we hope to meet the athletes in many a contest in the near future."[13]

At the top left in civilian clothes is Irving Mackay Glen, the team's organizer. He was a man of athletics, knowledge, and culture. Glen, who graduated from the University of Oregon in 1894, organized and managed the team shown here, won an oratorical prize in his senior year, joined the school's faculty in 1897, was chairman of three faculty committees—athletics, student affairs, and senior standing—led the university glee club, was dean of the school of music, and headed the university's department of early English language and literature.[14]

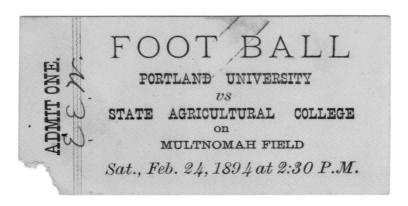

This ticket was for the first intercollegiate football contest played in Portland. The game was held on February 24, 1894, at Portland's Multnomah Field. In its first football game, the now-defunct Portland University gave Oregon Agricultural College its first loss of the season, winning 26–12. The Portland team "played with a snap and a dash that showed confidence in their own ability," according to the *Oregonian*, which added that playing conditions were a challenge that day: "The field was in a wretched condition, owing to the recent fall of snow. It was covered with about three inches of soft, sticky mud, surmounted by an inch of snow, and the landscape was relieved here and there by small lakes of clear, ice-cold water."[15]

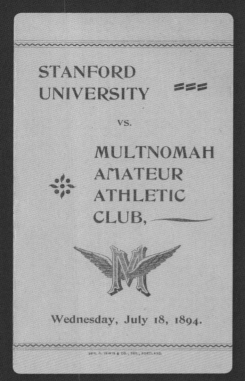

STANFORD
UNIVERSITY ===

VS.

MULTNOMAH
AMATEUR
ATHLETIC
CLUB, ———

Wednesday, July 18, 1894.

MRS. G. IRWIN & CO., PRS., PORTLAND.

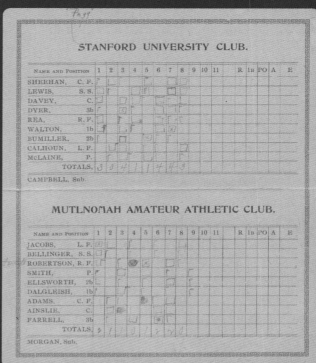

Less than two months after the Multnomah Amateur Athletic Club incorporated in 1891, W. L. Murray represented it in track events during games held at Portland's Armory. It was probably the first competitive appearance by a club athlete. That June, the MAAC fielded a baseball team against Company I of the Oregon National Guard in what was likely its first competitive team sport. Admission to the contest cost twenty-five cents. The club prevailed, and with the win captured Portland's amateur baseball championship.[16] The match was played at a new Portland baseball field between SE First and Second and Belmont and Morrison called The Oaks. A box reserved for the MAAC had been built into the grandstand.[17]

Two years later, the Multnomah Club leased the tract that became Multnomah Field, now Providence Park. "ATTENTION! Baseball, Football, Lawn Tennis, Bicycle Clubs, Sports and Amusements in General" was the headline to an 1893 newspaper advertisement announcing the lease. The ad aimed to spur public interest in the club and in renting the grounds.[18]

This score card was issued for a baseball game the club played there in 1894 against Stanford University. The Multnomahs lost 20–9 in a discouraging performance in which an estimated thousand spectators saw their 4–3 third-inning lead unravel. "Portland goes to pieces" is how the *Oregonian* summarized it. As for Stanford, "Their hits came with startling regularity, and were generally coupled pretty well with the Multnomahs' errors, which were always made about the time the visitors cared about scoring any runs."[19]

From the seventh game in University of Oregon football history comes this ticket—a 6–4 win over the now-defunct Portland University at Multnomah Field on November 16, 1895. In its game summary, the *Oregonian* described the scene:

> It was a fair crowd that saw the game from the stand and side lines. Fifteen hundred people passed the gate; but what they lacked in numbers they made up in enthusiasm, and the chorus of college yells and din of blaring fish-horns, kept up all through the game, at times drowned the voices of the captains as they gave out the signals. The bright crimson of Portland university was conspicuous in the grandstand, large numbers of the students having turned out to cheer their chrysanthemum-haired favorites on to victory. Many university girls were among the spectators, proudly wearing crimson streamers, and they applauded almost as heartily as the boys. The lemon yellow of the visitors was as much in evidence as the crimson, large numbers of graduates of the state university swelling the number of the delegation from Eugene, and it was questionable which team had the most admirers on the field.[20]

This mounted photo of three Albany football players dates to the 1896 era. Its photographer's pledge—"Hard times, but easy prices made by Long Photo Co."—appeared in Albany's *State Rights Democrat* on April 24, 1896. The players' ages suggest they may be from the Albany Collegiate Institute, which later became Portland's Lewis & Clark College.

MULTNOMAH AMATEUR ATHLETIC CLUB.

By-Laws and Rules Governing Use of Club House by Lady Members.

BY-LAWS.

1. Lady members shall have exclusive use of the Club House on Monday and Thursday mornings between the hours of 9 and 12 A. M. Between those hours, on the above days, all other members are prohibited from entering the Club House, or any part thereof, on any pretext whatever.

2. Tickets for Lady Members will be issued by the Secretary.

3. Each member of the Club will be entitled to secure tickets for any lady members of his family, the term "family" signifying mother, wife, sisters and daughters. Members not availing themselves of this privilege shall be entitled to secure a ticket for one lady friend.

4. Members desiring to procure tickets for ladies will make application to the Secretary or Superintendent on the printed blanks provided for that purpose.

5. All applications must be approved by the Board of Trustees before tickets can be issued by the Secretary.

6. The dues for Lady Members shall be $1.50 per month, payable monthly in advance. No initiation fee will be charged. Lady members are requested to pay their dues at the office of the Club on the first Monday of each month and will receive proper receipt therefor.

7. Ladies under 18 years of age are not eligible to membership.

8. Ladies accepting tickets will be considered as members until their resignations are tendered in writing, and all Ladies' tickets will be issued subject to this rule.

9. Ladies who may terminate their membership by resignation shall be ineligible for membership for the period of six months from the date of withdrawal.

10. Lady members will have free access to the Social Rooms, (not including Billiard Room) Gymnasium, Bath rooms, Swimming Pool, Bowling Alley and Hand Ball Court; also the use of Multnomah Field on Monday and Thursday mornings. On all other days they shall be permitted to have use of the Field at all hours as spectators only, excepting regular games or events when admission is charged.

11. Lady members having occasion to be absent from the city for a period of three months or longer may, by giving written notice to the Secretary, be classed as absent members and shall during such absence pay dues at rate of 25 cents per month.

RULES—GENERAL.

1. Lady members will be required to show their tickets at the Club door. The only entrance will be at the front door.

2. No visitors will be permitted in the Club House on Ladies' days.

3. Members are prohibited from giving any gratuities to any servant of the Club upon any pretext whatever.

4. Periodicals, newspapers or other publications belonging to the Club must not be removed from the Reading Room, nor cut, marked, or otherwise defaced.

5. No reprimand shall be given the servants or employees by members of the Club; but any lack of courtesy or attention to their duties must be reported to the Superintendent.

6. No person shall take from the Club House any article belonging to or in possession of the Club.

EDW. COOKINGHAM,
President.

7. No Dogs allowed in any part of the building.

8. No employee shall leave the Club House on the private business of any of the members.

9. Bathing suits must be used in the Swimming Pool.

10. Members must shower or sponge off before entering the Swimming Pool.

GYMNASIUM RULES.

1. While exercising members are required to wear gymnasium apparel, slippers, or light shoes without heels.

2. The wearing of finger rings while exercising is positively forbidden.

3. Members unacquainted with the use of the apparatus must apply to the Instructor or assistant for advice, and permission obtained before its use is attempted.

4. All movable apparatus must be used carefully, and at once returned to its place after using.

5. Any member damaging any piece or pieces of apparatus shall be liable to pay for the full extent of such damage.

6. Any person who may be careless in the use of gymnasium property shall be liable, on complaint, to suspension from Club privileges. All breakages must be reported at once to the Instructor.

7. Lady members who are not in gymnasium apparel will not be permitted on the gymnasium floor. The gallery in the gymnasium will be open for their use.

8. During the time that class instruction is being given no outside exercising will be permitted on the gymnasium floor.

BOWLING ALLEY.

1. A game shall consist of ten innings.

2. The cost of each game shall be at the rate of five cents for each participant, and the Captain of the losing side shall collect and make payment for the game.

3. The manner of payment shall be as follows: Tickets provided for that purpose, shall be signed by the Captain of the losing side, and the money handed to the person in charge.

4. Each game shall be paid for at its conclusion, before the pins are set up for the ensuing game.

5. No more than three games shall be bowled by the same parties successively, if others are waiting.

6. Persons desiring to bowl, if alleys are in use, will write their names upon a tablet provided for such purpose, and they will then bowl as their names appear.

7. Members are requested not to walk upon the alleys. Pitching and Lofting are positively prohibited.

8. To avoid serious accident players are cautioned against bowling while the pins are being set up.

9. The Superintendent is required to report any violation of these rules.

HAND BALL COURT.

1. 21 aces shall constitute a game.

2. No single match will be allowed to be played if a four-handed match is made.

3. Only three (3) games in succession are allowed, if another match is made.

4. Hand balls can be procured at the office at a cost of 40 cents each.

GEO. L. BICKEL,
Secretary.

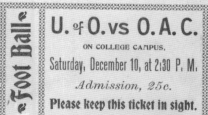

In 1896, the Multnomah Amateur Athletic Club issued a set of rules for its female members. On Mondays and Thursdays between nine and noon, "lady members" had the club to themselves, though they were not permitted in the billiard room and were "positively forbidden" from wearing rings on their fingers while exercising.

This 1898 ticket was for the sixth game in Civil War history between the University of Oregon and Oregon Agricultural College. Businesses closed during the game and a thousand fans attended. On a muddy field in Corvallis on December 10, 1898, OAC possessed the ball just twice and each time quickly turned it over on downs. The University of Oregon prevailed 38–0.[21]

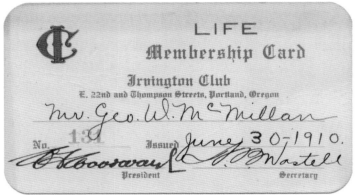

The 1899 Multnomah Amateur Athletic Club membership card belonged to future club president, George McMillan. In the 1890s, he played football for Stanford, Oakland's Reliance Athletic Club, and Montana's Butte and Anaconda teams. McMillan was a Stanford football coach for part of 1901, and he was variously a player, manager, captain, or coach for the Multnomah Club team from 1898–1909. He died in Portland on April 7, 1911, trying to climb between train boxcars. A "grand old football warrior," the *Oregon Daily Journal* called him.[22] He was also a lifetime member of Portland's Irvington Club, a tennis organization.

Multnomah Amateur Athletic Club football player George McMillan, circa 1901. (The same image of George McMillan was published in the *Oregonian* with an extensive caption about his life to that point.)[23]

The 1899 University of Oregon champions, apparently in track, are shown in this photo taken by the Winter Photo Company in Eugene. The images in the windows were added later and are presumably team members who were not present when the photograph was taken. "U of O Athletic Team, Champions of Oregon 1899," the caption states.

"Lents playground around 1900" reads a handwritten note on this cabinet photo of country baseball played in what is now a bustling southeast Portland neighborhood. The area was named for Oliver P. Lent. He was born in Ohio in 1830 and came overland to Oregon in 1852. Upon his death in 1899, the *Oregonian* described his impact on the area now called Lents: "Here he acquired much land, which he cleared and cultivated and opened up that district. . . . A good neighbor, a forceful, robust man, mentally and physically, he will not soon be forgotten, but will be classed among the pioneers who wrought the foundation of a great state."[24]

The Feldenheimer trophy, offered as a prize to the winner of the championship of the Inter-Scholastic Baseball League for 1900, goes to the Portland Academy nine, which has a record of seven victories and only one local defeat during the present season. The clever lads composing the team defeated the Portland High School nine, in the only two games played of the series between the two; the Bishop Scott Academy players, two out of three times; the Vancouver High School boys twice, and the Portland Dental College team in one game. They were defeated by the Bishop Scott youngsters in the contest of April 21.

What is presumably the Feldenheimer trophy sits on the table among the players. The Portland Academy was a college preparatory school that opened in 1889 and closed in 1916 when high school curricula expanded, reducing academy attendance.[25]

When a team name is too long to fit on a jersey, most clubs use an abbreviation, a few letters or a symbol, not an entire word. This 1900-era Clatskanie player squeezed his city's entire ten-letter name onto his uniform, resorting to a dash and what was probably an unintentionally reversed "N." Clatskanie had a baseball team by July 1896.[26]

At the center of this artful photo of the 1900 La Grande baseball team is its manager, William Klepper. He owned the Portland Beavers from winter 1921 through 1924, when he sold the team to Tom Turner (a Beavers scout) and John T. Shibe (part owner of the Philadelphia Athletics of the American League). In 1942, Klepper again obtained an ownership interest in the Beavers. He was the team's general manager when it won the 1945 pennant, but he declined a Bill Klepper Night at the stadium, preferring that the team and manager Marv Owen be given the honor. He was also the principal owner of the PCL's Seattle Rainiers club in 1919–1921 and 1927–1936.[27]

Joe Fay of the La Grande baseball team is pictured in 1900. Fay had a few at-bats with the 1906 Portland Beavers, and a more active stretch with the Beavers in 1907. In 1908, he coached the Oregon Agricultural College baseball team. Note the old-style baseball glove on his left hand.

TINKER, Third Base   DEISEL, Shortstop   SALISBURY, Pitcher   WEED, Right Field   ANDERSON, Second Base   MAHAFFEY, First Base
ENGLE, Pitcher   GLENDON, Pitcher   GRIM, Playing Manager   BROWN, Center Field   MULLER, Left Field
VIGNEUX, Catcher

PORTLAND BASEBALL CLUB, 1901

Future baseball Hall of Famer Joe Tinker (far left) and the Portland Webfoots team finished first in the Pacific Northwest League in 1901 over the Seattle Clamdiggers, Spokane Blue Stockings, and Tacoma Tigers. Tinker was in his second year of professional baseball. He then left Portland for the major leagues, playing from 1902–1916 with the Chicago Orphans, Chicago Cubs, Cincinnati Reds, and Chicago's Federal League entries.

Smash-mouth football? Not a problem for the team representing Portland's North Pacific Dental College in 1901. In 1945 the school became the Dental School of the University of Oregon, which later emerged as the Oregon Health & Science University School of Dentistry. In their 17–0 loss to Portland Academy at Multnomah Field on October 30, 1901, "the Academy goal was never seriously menaced, and the playing was confined largely to the tooth-carpenters' territory," the *Oregonian* reported.[28]

Ramsey Tennis Club.
Dufur, Ore.

The note on the back of this photo of a match in progress reads, "Tennis game near Coburg, June 1903." Oregon has a long tennis history. Lawn tennis supplies were among the sporting goods advertised in the *Eugene City Guard* as early as 1880. Oregon's first tennis champion was crowned in 1899. By 1912, tennis was popular enough that a Portland sporting goods store ran an ad for restringing tennis rackets.[29] The group postcard pictures the Ramsey Tennis Club of Dufur in around 1910. A comment on the back further explains, "This is part of our tennis club, taken last Sept. There were only a few of the members present. Flora."

Attend Our 4th Annual
MAY DAY BASKET
PICNIC

At Enegren's Grove To-morrow. BASEBALL; North Bend vs Marshfield, Purse $25. Games, Dancing; Music By Anderson's Orchestra. The Marshfield Band will attend. A good time is assured.

Fare including admission to the grounds 50 cents.

Fifty cents admitted guests to a 1904 May Day picnic on the Coos River that included a baseball game between North Bend and Marshfield (renamed Coos Bay in 1944). Marshfield's newspaper announced, "The North Bend Band will give an excursion and Basket Picnic up Coos River on Sunday, May 1st. A purse of $25 will be hung up for a baseball game between North Bend and Marshfield. There will also be other sports. Anderson's Orchestra will furnish music for dancing throughout the day, and a good time is assured to all who attend."[30]

A note on the back of the photo reads, "Ft. Stevens ball team, 04." The *Oregonian* reported on three of Fort Stevens' 1904 baseball games, all losses, to the Astoria Commercial Club, Fort Flagler (coast artillery from Puget Sound), and a Cathlamet, Washington team."[31]

Raymond Photo of Moro snapped these circa 1905 unidentified baseball images. The players are likely from Moro or a nearby town. "Red Kids" is the name on the jerseys of the two players. The single player leaning forward wears a different uniform.

The postcard of three female baseball players dates to about 1905. The back identifies the location as Houlton, which merged with St. Helens in 1913.[32] A note on the back asks, "Did the wagon break down again before you got home?" Their uniforms are a mash-up. The inside-out jersey of the player on the left probably reads South Bend (presumably in Washington State). "HO" seems to be the initials on the player's uniform in the center. On the right is a player wearing two different socks.

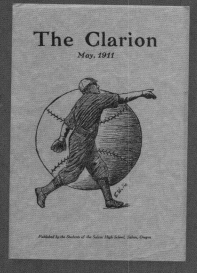
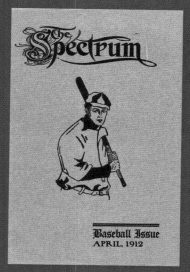
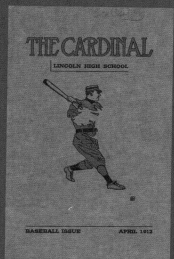

These wonderful high school yearbooks celebrate the baseball teams of, from left to right, Salem High (*The Clarion*, 1905); Portland's Washington High (*The Lens*, 1910); Salem High (*The Clarion*, 1911); and Portland's Jefferson High (*The Spectrum*, 1912), Lincoln High (*The Cardinal*, 1912), and Jefferson High (*The Spectrum*, 1914).

Pap Hayseed, whose less colorful real name was Harvey McAlister (top row, second from left), played center on the first four Oregon Agricultural College football teams from 1893–1896. In 1905, McAlister, by then a Spanish American War veteran, played center once more, this time for the school's football alumni in a game against the varsity team. The alumni, shown in this photograph, lost 10–6. "The playing of the old warriors was a feature, several performing in old time form," the *Oregon Daily Journal* reported.[33]

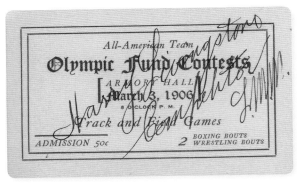

A national fundraising effort to send American athletes to compete in Athens in 1906 at the Intercalated Games—at the time they were regarded as the 1906 Olympics— included benefit games held at Portland's Armory on March 3, 1906. This ticket was issued to Harry Livingston, who took third in the senior 50-yard dash at the Armory while running for the Portland YMCA. Portland raised $700 for the cause. "The Athens team benefit games at the Armory last evening were a great success in every particular, for the large gathering present in the galleries heartily appreciated the efforts of the young gladiators who participated in the games on the floor of the drill hall and in the roped arena," the *Oregonian* reported on March 4. Portland athlete Herbert Kerrigan competed in Athens and brought home the bronze medal in the high jump.[34]

Portland's Vaughn Street Park, known in its early days as Recreation Park, opened in 1901 and saw baseball action through its last season in 1955. The park was home to Portland's professional ball clubs and was also used by local teams. The date of the game is likely 1905 because beyond the outfield fence are flags flying over buildings erected for the 1905 Lewis and Clark Centennial Exposition.

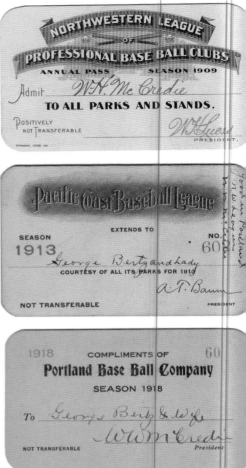

Walter McCredie led the Portland Beavers to Pacific Coast League pennants in 1906, 1910, 1911, 1913, and 1914. This photo was taken in Fresno, California, on April 5, 1906, two days before Portland's 1–0 opening game win there over the Fresno Raisin Eaters. He joined the Portland club in 1904, and at the end of the year obtained an ownership interest in it with his uncle, William Wallace McCredie. They gained sole ownership in December 1905.[35]

Walter was a Portland player, manager, or both from 1905 through 1921, except in 1918 when the PCL dropped Portland. He managed Salt Lake that year while Portland fielded a team called the Buckaroos in the Pacific Coast International League. Walter returned as the Beavers' manager from 1919–1921, and briefly in 1934, until he was replaced due to ill health. He died three months later. His uncle William was also the owner and president of a team Portland fielded in the Class B Northwestern League in 1909, and from 1911–1914.[36]

The three baseball passes are related to the three Portland teams. The 1909 pass for Northwestern League games belonged to Walter. The 1913 PCL pass bears a note from William. The 1918 pass is for Portland Buckaroos baseball games.

In the fifth and final athletic competition among Oregon National Guard companies in 1906, Company F (Third Infantry) was declared the year's overall best. Before one thousand spectators at Portland's Armory on May 21, the final day's events were the 50-yard dash, high jump, 440-yard dash, half-mile walk, tug of war, tent pitching, wall scaling, bayonet race, and relay.[37] This photograph shows Company F's winning relay team with a gold cup they were awarded.

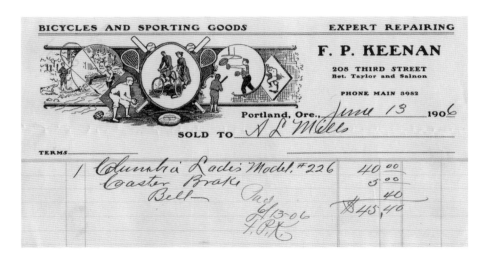

BICYCLES AND SPORTING GOODS   EXPERT REPAIRING

F. P. KEENAN

208 THIRD STREET
Bet. Taylor and Salmon

PHONE MAIN 3982

Portland, Ore., *June 13* 190*6*

SOLD TO *A L Mcee*

TERMS

1	Columbia Ladies Model #226	40 00
	Coaster Brake	5 00
	Bell	40
	Pd 6/13-06 F.P.K	$45.40

This nicely illustrated 1906 billhead from Portland's F. P. Keenan, dealer in bicycles and sporting goods, includes graphics of hunting, fishing, baseball, cycling, tennis, boxing, and football. Billheads combined advertising with a receipt for a purchase. The buyer of the Columbia Ladies' bicycle, brake, and bell was A. L. Mills, speaker of the Oregon House of Representatives in 1905, and later the president of the First National Bank of Portland.

"We are playing a good clean game of basket ball here," states this postcard of a woman in basketball attire sent to and from Independence on Christmas Day, 1906. Basketball, invented in 1891, was being played in Oregon by late 1893. From there the game rapidly ascended to become—and stay—one of the state's most popular sports.

The Dallas College team in the postcard won the 1906–1907 state basketball league title, but the squad from Oregon Agricultural College, though not in the league, claimed they were Oregon's best. On February 22, 1907, Dallas dealt Willamette University its first home loss by an Oregon team on a court "so small that the center circle and the foul-line circles overlapped."[38] The postcard of dorm life at Dallas College has an advertising poster for that Willamette game on the far left wall (the top poster of the two).

O.A.C. BASKET BALL TEAM, CHAMPIONS OF THE PACIFIC COAST, SCORE THIS YEAR 1128, OPPONENTS 304 CORVALLIS, ORE.

BILYEU
FORWARD

ROOPER

FOSTER
CENTRE

SWAN
FORWARD

REID

"OAC Basket Ball Team Champions of the Pacific Coast," asserts this postcard of the 1906–1907 Oregon Agricultural College men's team. They had a two-season winning streak broken by the Chicago Crescents in March 1907. That year Dallas College asserted that they, not OAC, were the state's top team, a claim OAC disputed, according to the *Oregonian*. Pictured from left are Hamon "Hame" Bilyeu, Henry "Heinie" Rooper, Walter "Shorty" Foster, Claude "Skeeter" Swan, and Nollie Reed (you don't need a nickname when your name is Nollie). The OAC yearbook added a rousing "yell" on the team's page: "Strawberry shortcake, blueberry pie, V-I-C-T-O-R-Y! Are we in it? Well, I guess! OAC Champions! Yes! Yes! Yes!"[39]

"Girls OAC Basket Ball Team. Undefeated Champions of Oregon,"
boasts this 1906–1907 Oregon Agricultural College team postcard.
The *Corvallis Gazette* praised both the men's and women's teams in
April 1907, when it advised that it was up to the OAC baseball team
to "make a reputation in keeping with records so far established the
past season by the basketball men and also by the basketball girls'
team at OAC."[40]

The University of Oregon football team's first forward pass came in its opening game of 1906, the year the play was made legal, in a 10–0 win on October 20 over the Astoria Football Club. "Oregon attempted the forward pass with poor success, making yardage upon this play only once during the game," the *Oregonian* reported. The outdoor postcard is of the 1906 Oregon team. Legendary trainer Bill Hayward stands in white. Coach Hugh Bezdek (hat, overcoat) sits in the first row, far left. A 1907 Astoria Football Club postcard is also shown.

July 7, 1907. Bonanza, Oregon, Merrill Baseball

The Merrill baseball team, pictured in this postcard, has ball and five bats brought to nearby Bonanza for a game on July 7, 1907. Small town baseball was common in Oregon in the early 1900s. In February 1908, the Klamath Falls *Evening Herald* reported, "The fine spring weather has caused the baseball fever to rise in the veins of the Merrill batters, and the young men may be seen almost any day practicing on the baseball grounds."[42]

J. A. McHolland. Champion of the Seaside Alleys. Score 264. 1907.

The postcard's inscription reads "J. A. McHolland, Champion of the Seaside Alleys, Score 264, 1907." The *Oregonian* explained in 1913, "The breaking of a record here at Seaside is one of the many diversions of Summer visitors."[43] McHolland's score is also written on the ball.

5222 O. A. C. FOOTBALL TEAM, CORVALLIS, OREGON, PACIFIC COAST CHAMPIONS 1907.
TOP ROW BEGINNING AT LEFT, GREENHAW, MGR. BENNETT, BARBER, SMITH, DUNLAP,
KELLY, JAMISON, PENDERGRASS, NORCROSS, COACH. SECOND ROW, LOONEY, WOLFF,
COOPER, EMILY, THIRD ROW, DOBLIN, GAGNOW, RHEINHARDT, CADY.

A perfect 6–0 record while outscoring the opposition 137–0 is the outstanding feat achieved by this 1907 Pacific Coast football championship Oregon Agricultural College team. Their victories included a 4–0 win over the University of Oregon in the Civil War game; they capped off the season with a 10–0 shutout over the previously undefeated St. Vincent's College of Los Angeles.[44]

The Canby baseball club entered the 1907 season as the Clackamas County champion, according to the *Oregon City Courier*. The club beat Gresham 1–0 in fourteen innings on May 19, the record at that date for the longest shut-out game played in Oregon. According to the *Oregonian,* "The Canby team is willing to play any good amateur team in Oregon or Washington."[45]

The ball is marked "08 M.S.C." and the postmark is Sodaville, where Mineral Springs College was located, leading to the conclusion that this postcard portrays the school's 1908 basketball team. The image is interesting for its scarcity—the college closed in 1908—along with the inspired hairstyles of the two players in the center.[46]

These postcards show two of Oregon's 1908 non-conference football teams, that year's champion Albany College and rival Pacific University. The other non-conference teams were Willamette University and the Chemawa Indian School.[47] Their uniforms, minimal by today's standards, include nose guards hanging from the necks of the two Albany players on either side of the ball, and headgear with openings.

U of I 21
U of O. 27

#4   Idaho advancing the ball and Oregon about to tackle.

Dateline Moscow, Idaho, October 31, 1908: "In the most sensational football game ever seen in the Pacific Northwest the inexperienced Oregon eleven today defeated Idaho by the score of 27 to 21." The Idaho fan who sent this postcard added a succinct message of defiance: "They beat us six points but we outplayed them." They played in the Pacific Northwest Intercollegiate Conference, with the University of Washington winning the 1908 title over the University of Oregon, Oregon Agricultural College, Washington State University, Whitman College, and the University of Idaho.[48]

O. A. C. vs. OREGON
Multnomah Field, Portland, November 21, 1908

Captain Wolff

Captain Moullen

UNIVERSITY
OF OREGON

OREGON

YELL
Rah! Rah! Rah!
Rah! Rah! Rah!
Rah! Rah! Rah!
University of Oregon

The underdog University of Oregon team won the 1908 Civil War football game 8–0 over rival Oregon Agricultural College. Ten thousand people watched in Portland's Multnomah Stadium, and more than five thousand saw what they could from vantage points outside the venue. Eugene rooters tossed green confetti, and Corvallis fans improvised orange megaphones from cardboard sheets. Most fans wore their preferred team's colors and insignia, and college songs and yells filled the air.[49] The 1910-era poster stamp offers a stirring U of O yell: "Rah! Rah! Rah! "Rah! Rah! Rah! "Rah! Rah! Rah! University of Oregon."

Three Oregon track and field stars medaled at the 1908 London Olympics. Gold went to Alfred Gilbert in the pole vault (he invented the Erector set) and Forrest Smithson in the 110-meter hurdles. They were Oregon's first Olympic gold medalists. Daniel Kelly took silver in the running broad jump (the long jump). *Oregonian* ads in 1908 promoted "Special Postal Cards" of "Oregon's Champions of the World, Smithson, Gilbert, and Kelly" that the Boyer Printing Company published.[50] What is believed to be a full set is shown here. Images of the Oregon winners include a New York City ceremony to bestow medals, congratulations from then-President Theodore Roosevelt, and a photo with Lipton Tea founder Sir Thomas Lipton.

The Pendleton Pets team in this postcard played in the 1908 Inland Empire
League with the Baker City Nuggets, La Grande Babes, and a Walla Walla
team. The IEL lasted for just one season. Before the league was organized,
Pendleton was to play in La Grande, but their games were delayed by a week
for an unusual reason, reported the *Evening Observer*:

> The baseball series scheduled with Pendleton in this city, to commence Thursday
> and end Friday, has been postponed by mutual consent, due to the fact that the
> carpenters failed to complete the grandstand, and the local promoters did not
> wish to break the grounds in until everything is in readiness. Just when the
> Pendleton game will be pulled off here depends on the alacrity with which the
> contractors complete their work. The frequent rains of late are deterring comple-
> tion considerably.

League games later began, and by July, with La Grande ahead of the rest, the
season concluded due to excessive heat and falling attendance in Pendleton.[51]

Gracing this postcard is Harry Gardner, a brief major leaguer with the Pittsburgh Pirates, who in 1908 led Coquille to the Coos County Baseball League pennant over Marshfield, North Bend, and Bandon.[52]

Hall of Famer Cy Young pitched in the major leagues from 1890–1911. Due to his longevity and skill, his pitching records include total wins, losses, and complete games. Notes on this 1908 postcard of "Old" Cy—he was forty-one then—refer to his brother Otto in Elgin. Elgin held a banquet for Cy attended by forty people when he visited his brother in February 1910.[53] Accompanying the caption, "The things that OLD 'Cy' didn't do, made him famous," are images suggesting he did not drink, carouse, or gamble on card games or horse racing.

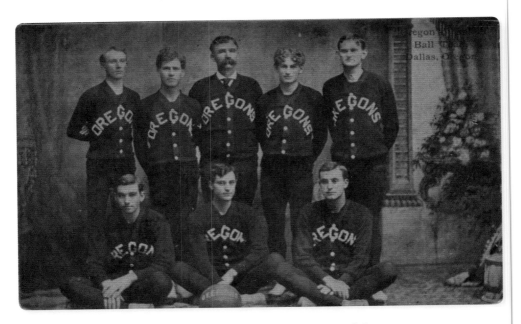

"Dallas Basket-Ball Team to Advertise Oregon in East," stated the *Oregonian's* headline in 1908 above the image in this postcard. The caption read, in part:

> The Oregons' basketball team, representing the city of Dallas, will start early
> next week on a tour of the states of the East and Middle West. While en [*sic*]
> tour they will play 52 games. The team will be supplied with literature adver-
> tising the City of Dallas and setting forth the resources of the surrounding
> country, which will be distributed in every city and town through which the
> team passes. The plan was inaugurated by the business men of this city for the
> purpose of advertising Dallas, and the team is to be financed on its tour by funds
> contributed by the commercial interests of the city.

They ultimately played fifty-eight games in nineteen states, won forty-
nine of them (including the game this ticket was for, a 55–14 road win over
Spokane's YMCA team), lost eight, and tied one.[54]

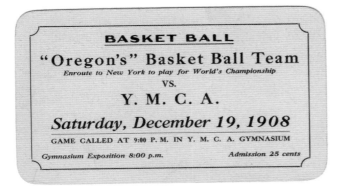

BASKET BALL

"Oregon's" Basket Ball Team

Enroute to New York to play for World's Championship

VS.

Y. M. C. A.

Saturday, December 19, 1908

GAME CALLED AT 9:00 P. M. IN Y. M. C. A. GYMNASIUM

Gymnasium Exposition 8:00 p.m.   Admission 25 cents

First Row: Horton, Augh, Hamilton, Spinis, Moore.
Back Row: Rud, Keck, Cooper and Heater, trainer.

The Oregon Agricultural College basketball team won the 1908–1909 intercollegiate championship of Oregon with a 16–15 victory over Whitman College in Walla Walla on February 26, 1909. Whitman entered the game having won the intercollegiate championships of Washington and Idaho. "The game was played at a dizzy pace, Whitman outplaying the visitors in the first half, but failing to maintain the standard in the second. Many of the goals thrown were spectacular, both squads displaying a high system of team work," the *Oregonian* reported. There were differing and competing basketball rules then, those of the Amateur Athletic Union and also intercollegiate rules. This OAC team played the first basketball game in the Northwest under intercollegiate rules on January 16, 1909.[55]

A gentleman in a Scio uniform crouches before the Woodburn Blue Birds baseball team of the Tri-City League in a postcard likely from 1908. A note on the back of the 1909 "The Lions" of Scio postcard of female players reads, "This team beat the Star Nine 3 to 1 in a 5-inning game." The *Oregonian* had previewed the contest: in Scio, "a unique feature of the carnival of sports to be held here the latter part of this week will be a baseball game next Saturday afternoon between two teams composed entirely of girls. A number of local girls have been practicing strenuously for the contest and it will be an interesting exhibition."[56]

The center for Astoria High School's women's basketball team is featured on a postcard mailed in February 1909 to William E. Gregory, Captain of the *USS Armeria*, detailing past and future games. The team disbanded in November 1909 after the coach insisted they play under girls' rules; the team countered that other teams would only play them under boys' rules.[57]

The first Civil War game between the University of Oregon and Oregon State University was played in 1894 in baseball, not football. Irving Mackay Glen, the organizer and manager of that University of Oregon team (shown earlier in the book), stands in the upper right of this circa 1909 postcard, hand in pocket. An interesting story about UO baseball comes from 1879, when the team beat Junction City in Eugene 22–19. The *Eugene City Guard* explained, "A considerable amount of wrangling characterized the game, caused from all appearances, by that promoter of discord, spts. frumenti."[58] ("Spts. frumenti" is short for spiritus frumenti: whiskey.)

The generic drawings of female basketball players on these postcards accurately reflect that the sport, invented in 1891, was popular among women and men. The two-player card was mailed from Blachly in 1909. The card depicting a lone player in Oregon Agricultural College orange beneath an OAC pennant was sent from Corvallis in 1911.

A mix of players wearing jerseys of Prineville and what probably says Redmond gather in this 1909 postcard. The image may be related to a best-of-three series between them played in Prineville and won by the home team two games to one, with each contest being decided by only one run. "Both teams done snappy playing, remarkably free from errors, and every man was up on his toes from start to finish," the *Crook County Journal* reported.[59]

These images of 1909-era Banks baseball offer a study in contrasts. Players relax under the casual gaze of family or friends on the porch in one, and are prepared to do battle under the restless watch of fans in the grandstand in the other.[60]

A Scotts Mills player shows his reach in this 1909 postcard. The message reads, "Here is S.M. center fielder this season when he is not in the [pitcher's] box. Last Sat. I fanned down [struck out] several of the boys here. They are going to give me a chance at pitching some this summer on the way I through [*sic*: throw] it fools them when they are coming [batting]."

Unidentified players in a postcard mailed from St. Helens, 1909.

The 1909 postcard of Kerby baseball players is unique because their positions on the diamond are inscribed on their caps—visible are SS (short stop), 3B (third baseman), C (catcher), and P (pitcher). In 1873, Salem's College Club team displayed their on-field positions on their belts. "The College boys will wear a uniform of white shirts with blue cuffs, collar and shield—with red letter in shield—silk caps, and belts on which the name of club and position each player holds is painted."[61]

With the popularity of organized athletics in Oregon came sporting goods purveyors, some of which sponsored baseball teams. Portland Gun & Bicycle Co. backed one in 1909, as seen on the jersey of the player wearing the "Portland G&B Co." uniform. In 1911, Portland's H. T. Hudson Arms Co.'s nine won its first eighteen of nineteen ball games.[62] The message on the postcard of the player outfitted in their uniform explained, "Here is my husband in his ball suit[—]it looks just like him. Of course he looks a little different in his other clothes."

POST CARD

CORRESPONDENCE HERE | NAME AND ADDRESS HERE

Cooston Baseball
team vs. North Bend
Sunday the 25 of April
boat leaves Cooston
10 a.m. for North
Bend. come and
see, it will be
a good one,
VL,

Miss Anna Wyatt,
North Bend,
Oregon.

Miss Anna Wyatt was invited into a hornet's nest of controversy when the sender of this postcard suggested that she would see "a good one" if she took the 10 a.m. Sunday boat from Cooston to North Bend for an April 25, 1909, baseball game. The contest reportedly ended in a nine-inning, nine-to-nine tie. Not content to let numerical perfection stand, the teams agreed to reconvene two weeks later. Then the press spilled some ink. April 26: press report of the game. April 27: press report of a North Bend player claiming that his team had actually won 8–7 and insisting that Cooston admit the loss as a prerequisite to a rematch. April 30: Cooston let everyone know what they thought of that idea. Fences had mended enough by July 4 celebrations in Cooston for baseball teams from the two towns to play a game. Cooston prevailed, though it is unknown if the game involved the same teams that had been enmeshed in the stalemate. Perhaps one of the spectators that day was Miss Anna Wyatt.[63]

Baseball teams in the early twentieth century sometimes had mascots, including children and animals. A uniformed child mascot highlights a 1909 postcard of the Hubbard team. "So far the Hubbard Whites have played nine games, and have lost but one. The team is one of the best amateur aggregations in the Willamette Valley."[64]

WONE
16 GAMES   ONTARIO. OREGON. BASE. BALL. TEAM.   LOST. 1.
                    PLAYED. 17. GAMES.

Usually baseball uniforms are just that: uniform. Apparently nobody told the unidentified players in the "P" jerseys postcard to affix the letter in the same spot, or that the entire team should wear one. The message on the reverse reads, "Dear Ma, I will be out Sun, if it don't rain. I am going to bring the boys that I work with out with me. We are coming out to shoot squirrels and have some fun. Be sure you have something good to eat. Have some chicken and noodle soup. That's my favorite. Willie." It was mailed to Cornelius from Portland in 1909. The message on the reverse of the undated Ontario postcard is more poignant: "Please keep this in spit[e] of anything as this is the only one he had left and we will keep it always."

Written in chalk over Camas (Washington) in the postcard with the scoreboard is "Grocers," and below that what appears to read "Salesmen" as the opponent, with the grocers losing 9–7. The scoreboard and Grocers Association team postcard were acquired together. The ninth annual picnic of the Portland Retail Grocers Association was held in 1909 in Camas, and included a baseball game between the grocers and traveling salesmen. A subsequent news report of the gathering gives a 9–8 Grocers' loss, but that is likely a typographical error because that same article's game write-up points to a 9–7 outcome, the result on the scoreboard.[65] The various uniforms of the players standing by the scoreboard suggests they were grocers or salesmen who played for other teams and wore those outfits for the game, or perhaps they were present for a different game and the earlier results had not been erased.

SATURDAY BALL GAME, OREGON STATE PENITENTIARY

"Dear L., this is a picture of our ball team. Many thanks for the basket of fruit," is the message on the back of a 1909 Oregon State Penitentiary team postcard. Was it sent by a prisoner? A guard? A Salem resident? Their opponents included a team of guards in 1908, the Chemawa Indian School in 1910, and Willamette University in 1911.[66] The player in the center is African American, not entirely uncommon in that era with local teams, but which would not occur in the major leagues until Jackie Robinson desegregated baseball in 1947. Also shown is a postcard of a Saturday baseball game at the penitentiary during the 1910 era.

A baseball sails past the head of the photographer, B. B. Bakowski, in a postcard of a game between Bend and Prineville at a September 6–8, 1909, tournament in Prairie City. The contest, open to any team in Eastern Oregon, had $600 in prize money at stake: $300 for the winner, $200 for second place, and $100 for third ("prosperous and enterprising" Prairie City had raised the money in one hour).[67] A bearded Canyon City player passes first base against Austin in the other postcard, one also taken by Bakowski at the tournament. Bakowski went missing in February 1911 after going to Crater Lake to take photographs.

This vexing postcard evades a definitive identification . . . but there are clues. It was sent from and to Corvallis on July 27, 1909. The players are wearing jerseys that appear to have a "C" on them. It seems safe to say it is a Corvallis team, but which one? There was a Corvallis High School team, but these players are older. Oregon Agricultural College had a baseball program, but they wore different attire. A local team called the Corvallis Cubs played there in 1909. The Cubs also received new uniforms on June 19, and the outfits in this postcard mailed on July 27 look fresh. The best that can be said is this is *probably* the Cubs, a team whose opponents that season included Junction City, a team of "post-office stamp-lickers," the Siletz Indians, and Elk City.[68]

"Oregon Forever; OAC Never" was the rallying cry seen on posters affixed to telephone poles around Eugene before the fourteenth Civil War game at Kincaid Field between the University of Oregon and Oregon Agricultural College in 1909. The Ducks prevailed 12–0.[69] This nicely illustrated twenty-five-cent souvenir program is from that game.

Bill Hayward, the University of Oregon's athletic trainer and track coach, after whom Hayward Field is named, stands wearing a cap at the far left of this postcard of the 1909 University of Oregon football team. (See page 193 for an image of the first game at the "new" Hayward Field in 1919.) Standing at the far right in a dark sweater is Oregon's coach Robert Forbes. In a 1906 game against Harvard while playing football for Yale, Forbes caught a forward pass in the first year it was legal to throw one. His catch set up the winning score in a game that arguably brought Yale the national championship. Player Bill Main, kneeling in the second row, fourth from the left, mailed this postcard on November 13, 1909, the day of Oregon's 22–6 win over Idaho at Portland's Multnomah Field.[70]

The 1909 Eugene High School football team in the postcard expected to vie for the Western Oregon interscholastic championship (they had won it two years earlier). They did not disappoint, beating every high school they played in 1909 after losing their first game 18–0 to the University of Oregon freshmen squad. Unsettled claims for the 1909 state title were asserted by Eugene High and by Portland's undefeated Washington High School team.[71]

Portland White Sox

"Portland White Sox" is the caption of the 1909 Portland Beavers postcard,
referring to manager Walter McCredie having ordered uniforms with white
stockings like those worn by the Chicago White Sox.[72] Those socks are not in
the "White Sox" image, but they are worn in the other postcard of the team,
which finished second in the Pacific Coast League in 1909.

1911 Obak cigarette cards:
Portland Beavers, Pacific Coast League

BARRY, PORTLAND, P. C. L.

CHADBOURNE, PORTLAND, P. C. L.

FULLERTON, PORTLAND, P. C. L.

HENDERSON, PORTLAND, P. C. L.

KOESTNER, PORTLAND, P. C. L.

KRUEGER, PORTLAND, P. C. L.

KUHN, PORTLAND, P. C. L.

McCREDIE, PORTLAND, P. C. L.

1911 Obak cigarette cards (*continued*): Portland Beavers, Pacific Coast League

MURRAY, PORTLAND, P. C. L.

PECKINPAUGH, PORTLAND, P. C. L.

RAPPS, PORTLAND, P. C. L.

RODGERS, PORTLAND, P. C. L.

J. RYAN, PORTLAND, P. C. L.

SEATON, PORTLAND, P. C. L.

SHEEHAN, PORTLAND, P. C. L.

STEEN, PORTLAND, P. C. L.

1911 Obak cigarette cards:

Portland Pippins, Northwestern League

BLOOMFIELD, PORTLAND, N. W. L.

CASEY, PORTLAND, N. W. L.

GARRETT, PORTLAND, N. W. L.

HARRIS, PORTLAND, N. W. L.

LAMLINE, PORTLAND, N. W. L.

MENSOR, PORTLAND, N. W. L.

MUNDORFF, PORTLAND, N. W. L.

SPEAS, PORTLAND, N. W. L.

STOVALL, PORTLAND, N. W. L.

WILLIAMS, PORTLAND, N. W. L.

McCredie. Portland

Peckinpaugh, ss. Portland

Rapps, 1b. Portland

Rapps, 1b., Portland.

Seaton, p. Portland

Steen, p. Portland

1911 Pacific Coast Biscuit cards:
Portland Beavers, Pacific Coast League

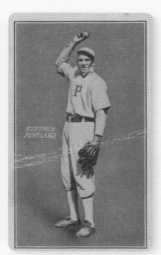

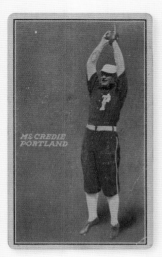

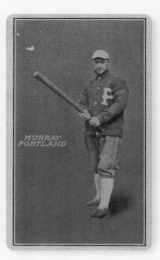

CHADBOURNE, Portland

HARKNESS, Portland

HENDERSON, Portland

KUHN, Portland

McCREDIE, Portland

MURRAY, Portland

PECKINPAUGH, Portland

RAPPS, Portland

RYAN, Portland

SEATON, Portland

SHEEHAN, Portland

STEEN, Portland

1911 Mono cigarette cards: Portland Beavers, Pacific Coast League

Gene Knapp, Port.

Chadbourn, Port.

R. Peckinpaugh, Port.

Wm. Stein, Port.

1911 Western Playground cards:
Portland Beavers, Pacific Coast League

1911 Obak cabinet photo:
Portland Beavers, Pacific Coast League

Both 1910-era postcards picture players from West Astoria, another name for the city's Uniontown area. The less formal one includes two athletes with "Brown's" jerseys, which may refer to the Astoria Browns team named for their manager Fred Brown.[75]

The clue to identifying this photo comes from a note on the reverse: "Ernest Lafky's football team in Salem." Period news accounts mention two Lafky players on the Salem High School team in 1907, and one in 1910 and 1911.[76] While a precise date cannot be assigned to the image from these facts, it is safe to conclude that it is the Salem High team in that era.

The Portland Cricket Club soccer team, known as the Cricketers, is likely the team shown on this postcard that was mailed in 1910. They competed in a Portland Football Association League composed of five teams: the Multnomah Amateur Athletic Club (which won the 1910 championship), the Cricketers, and teams called Queen's Park, Nationals, and Oceanics. The Cricketers finished the season with a winning 4–2–2 record.[77]

Junction City baseball team postcard, circa 1910.

One player wears a Hermiston uniform and the rest have "H" jerseys in this 1910-era postcard. No writing or postmark ties it to Oregon, but the only Hermiston in the United States is in Umatilla County. In 1910, that county's population was just 20,309, yet nine of its twelve now-incorporated cities had teams in local leagues over 1910 and 1911. Of those nine locales, Hermiston won the Irrigation League pennant in 1910 over Umatilla, Stanfield, and Echo. Weston claimed the Blue Mountain League crown in 1910 ahead of Athena, Pendleton, and Pilot Rock. Athena won that league's 1911 title by beating out Weston, Pendleton, Echo, Milton Freewater, and Walla Walla, Washington. In the three cities without league teams, local baseball was still played; in Adams and Helix in 1910 and 1911, and in Ukiah by 1911.[78]

A Mt. Angel college player swings through the ball thrown by an unknown opponent in this 1910-era postcard. One of the teams they played in that era was Salem's Chemawa Indian School. An account in the *Weekly Chemawa American* recounted the idyllic journey from Salem to Mt. Angel for a 1910 game that was won 3–2 by the home team:

> The baseball team left Chemawa on Wednesday morning at 8 o'clock sharp bound for Mt. Angel College to fill an engagement to play that team their last game of the season of 1910. The journey from Chemawa to Mt. Angel is a delightful drive, passing through a part of the Willamette Valley that shows what it is possible to produce in this very fertile country. On each side of the road are fields of grain, orchards of fruit, vineyards, and comfortable houses surrounded by beautiful flowers. At 10:15 we arrived at the stables of Mt. Angel College, which are situated at the foot of the college hill, distant about one-half mile from the main building.[79]

College Football Hall of Famer Bill Warner, coach of the University of Oregon football team in 1910 and 1911, stands with hands on his hips as he observes kicking practice. He later practiced law in Hermiston.[80] Also in the College Football Hall of Fame is his more famous brother, legendary coach Glenn Scobey "Pop" Warner.

Bergman – Cap't. O.A.C. Track Team

On April 16, 1910, the *Oregonian* published this image of the track star from OAC, noting that

> Captain Henry Bergman, of the Oregon Agricultural College track team, will be the mainstay of the supporters of the Orange at the Columbia meet today. Captain Bergman is a senior in the school of engineering and hails from Gardiner, Or. He won the senior championship in both high and low hurdles at the A.A.U. [Amateur Athletic Union] track and field meet, held at the A-Y-P [Alaska-Yukon-Pacific] Exposition in Seattle last Summer, competing with some of the premier hurdlers in the amateur ranks. Bergman will enter the 50 and 220-yard dashes, the hurdles, and will be a member of the OAC relay team.

OAC took second in the track meet to the University of Oregon, but Bergman had the highest individual point total with three second-place finishes.[86]

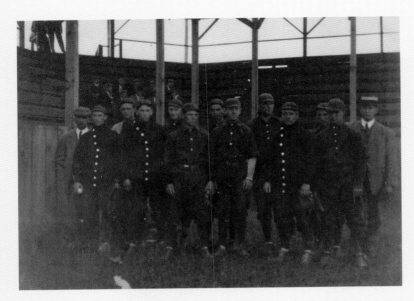

Oregon Agricultural College won the 1910 Northwest intercollegiate baseball pennant with a 10–4 win over the University of Oregon in eight innings. The *Oregonian* explained why the ninth inning was not played: "The varsity men [from the University of Oregon], convinced that they could not overcome the lead, asked that the game be called in order that they might catch the train."[87] Fielder Jones (far right) coached the OAC team. He played major league baseball for Brooklyn, the Chicago White Sox, and briefly for the Federal League's St. Louis Terriers.

The high schools of Marshfield and North Bend competed for the Coos County football championship on November 12, 1910, with Marshfield prevailing 6–5. "MARSHFIELD 1910 CHAMPS" trumpeted the front page of the *Coos Bay Times*. "The game was clean throughout and the rivals never once forgot that modern football is a gentleman's game."[88]

Pennants for Portland and Oregon, baseball gloves, a catcher's mask, baseballs, a bat, the Spalding baseball guide, and a tennis racket are among the offerings displayed in an unidentified store's window in this undated postcard. Some of the 1910-era baseball gloves had individual fingers. In the third-floor sporting goods department of Portland's Meier & Frank department store in 1909, a boy's flannel baseball uniform could be had for $1.15, baseball stockings for 29 cents, a baseball mitt for 39 cents, and a baseball for 19 cents.[89]

1036 — MULTNOMAH CLUB, PORTLAND, OREGON.

The Multnomah Amateur Athletic Club was located at SW Eighteenth Avenue and Morrison from 1900 until fire destroyed it in July 1910. Baseball players stand at its near corner. A new clubhouse built on Salmon between Eighteenth and Twentieth Avenues opened in 1912. President Theodore Roosevelt, the figure in the hat striding toward the camera at the far left of the bottom image, came to the site to lay the cornerstone for the new building on April 5, 1911, as seen in the postcard with an American flag and an even larger banner of the club's winged "M" emblem.

Portland Cricket Team 1910

The Portland Cricket Club opened the 1910 season on April 16 on their grounds at North Mount Tabor. "As usual a large number of the fair sex is expected to be present in the pavilion, where tea will be served between innings," the *Oregonian* noted. The image on this postcard was taken in 1910 in Victoria, British Columbia, at an international tournament.[90]

Cricket has a long history in and around Portland. A cricket match followed a July 4, 1867, baseball game in Oregon City. In July 1873, a cricket club was formed in Portland. They had to send away for equipment. The *Oregonian* reported, "By the steamer *Ajax* there arrived all the necessary paraphernalia for the Club. This consists of three bats, three balls, two pair of gauntlets, and two pair of leg guards. The wickets did not arrive, but these will be made in the city, as they are of very simple mechanism." The newspaper added that their upcoming play would represent the "first time in the city" for the game. They called themselves the St. George Cricket Club, had a constitution and bylaws, practices, and grounds to compete on. [91]

Sometimes just a few clues can reveal the facts. "Off to Albany April 14th, 1:00 p.m. Arrived at 3:00 p.m. and lost the game 6 to 5," says a note on the back of this postcard. A team of horses is shown about to transport unidentified players to an unspecified destination from beside a nameless sporting goods store in an unknown town. The two individuals standing at the far left hold baseballs. That was enough to unpack the scene. On April 14, 1911, Albany High School opened its baseball season with a 6–5 win over Corvallis High School in an afternoon game played on the Albany College baseball grounds. Corvallis erased a 6–0 deficit with a five-run sixth inning, but Albany held on for the victory. [92]

A Falls City Commercial Club player stands next to, presumably, his mother. The postcard is not identified as being from Oregon, but a photo of the Falls City Commercial Club team in a 1911 *Oregonian* issue appears to include this same player. The caption accompanying that image states, "The Falls City Commercial Club has adopted a novel form of advertising the resources of Falls City by organizing a baseball team. Falls City expects to be in line for state honors, as they have increased their strength by the addition of four new men."[93]

Hillsboro vs. Cornelius
Apr 29" 1911
Score 4 to 2 Cornelius — Hillsboro at bat

Opening game Hillsboro vs. Cornelius
Apr 29" 1911

The Hillsboro Cardinals lost their 1911 home opener 4–2 to the Cornelius Cubs at Athletic Realty Grounds. Cornelius won the Washington County Baseball League pennant that year with a 12–2 record over Hillsboro, a team from Banks, and the Forest Grove Colts. As for the timing of the season's end, "The cause of the annulment of further games was the fact that the teams were not getting the support they enjoyed earlier in the season—and the season was too lengthy, anyway."[94] The postcards of the Cardinals ("H" jerseys) and Cubs are from 1911.

794 A. M. BALL GAME 7-4-19-- CHAUTAUQUA ASSEMBLY
GLADSTONE PARK OREGON

Speakers, musicians, instructors, lecturers, entertainers, and baseball delighted the celebrants attending the 1911 Willamette Valley Chautauqua at Gladstone Park. This postcard shows the morning baseball game on July 4 between the Blackstones—a team composed of lawyers, dentists, ministers, and physicians— and the Teachers. At least five thousand people saw the Teachers down the Blackstones. "Although defeated fairly, the lawyers did considerable quibbling and once asked that the game be forfeited to them on a technicality," the *Oregonian* reported, very likely with a tongue firmly in cheek. [95]

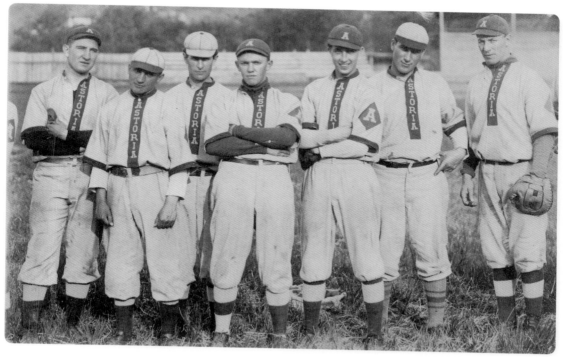

Two future major leaguers appear with the Astoria Giants in this 1912 postcard. Howie Haworth, center, played briefly with the Cleveland Indians in 1915. Rudy Kallio, third from right, played for the Detroit Tigers in 1918 and 1919, and for the Boston Red Sox in 1925.

Knights of Columbus No. 678 Baseball Team, 1912.

"With a record of eight wins in twelve games, the Knights of Columbus baseball team, led by Manager Joe Reilly, has no reason to feel disappointed in its initial season's record," the Oregonian declared in November 1912 about the Portland amateur team. With that reputation they traveled to Salem in 1913 as the opponent of the Salem Senators. "The K of C baseball club, one of the very best semipro ball teams in Portland, will play the Salem Senators May 4 in the opening game at league grounds. If you miss it you'll be sorry," Salem's Daily Capital Journal advised. The anticipation of contrition by those who missed the game was correct, as the Knights scored the game-winning run on one of the most exciting plays in baseball, a steal home, to earn a 2–0 victory. Salem could hold its head high, though, for the Knights' pitcher was a member of the Portland Beavers Pacific Coast League team, Al Carson. "He was engaged for yesterday's game only by the KC Boys, who paid a fat price for his services," the Daily Capital Journal reported. So goes the price of victory.99

These circa 1912 postcards show the Multnomah Amateur Athletic Club overlooking the south end of Multnomah Field, and the interior of the club's gymnasium. The field, currently called Providence Park, has been the home to college football games, including Civil War contests between the University of Oregon and Oregon State University; the first overtime National Football League game (an August 28, 1955, preseason contest between the New York Giants and Los Angeles Rams); and even an Elvis Presley concert in 1957.

"Sheets of rain and hailstones the size of marbles beat down upon the sawdust-capped rathskeller during the third quarter, but for all that the game was spectacular to the extreme," the *Oregonian* colorfully reported about a November 9, 1912, football game between the defending 1911 Northwest champion team, the University of Washington, and Oregon Agricultural College at Portland's Multnomah Field. The University of Washington prevailed 9–3 before a crowd of nearly four thousand.[100] The Multnomah Amateur Athletic Club sits above the south goal in this postcard of play during the game.

The Weed, California, team defeated Klamath Falls 9–3 and Fort Klamath 10–5 at a 1912 tournament in Klamath Falls on its way to winning the championship of Northern California and Southern Oregon.[101] Grants Pass native Ken Williams (fourth from left) played for Weed, was later with the Portland Beavers, and had a successful major league career with the Cincinnati Reds, St. Louis Browns, and Boston Red Sox.

TOP ROW, LEFT TO RIGHT

McCREDIE   STEIGER   HAWLEY   TEMPLE   LALONGE
    GILLIGAN   HENDERSON   LINDSAY   KOESTNER   KREUGER

BOTTOM ROW, LEFT TO RIGHT

HARKNESS   McDOWELL   ROGERS   CHADBOURNE   RAPPS   BANCROFT   LAMLINE

(OVER)

SAN FRANCISCO	PORTLAND'S	VERNON
April 16, 17, 18, 19, 20, 21. July 9, 10, 11, 12, 13, 14. Sept. 24, 25, 26, 27, 28, 29.	**BASEBALL** SCHEDULE 1912	April 30, May 1, 2, 3, 4, 5. July 16, 17, 18, 19, 20, 21. Aug. 27, 28, 29, 30, 31 Sept. 1, 2, a. m., p. m.
SACRAMENTO	OAKLAND	LOS ANGELES
May 28, 29, 30 a. m. p. m., 31, June 1, 2. July 23, 24, 25, 26, 27, 28. August 20, 21, 22, 23 24, 25	April 23, 24, 25, 26 27, 28. June 11, 12, 13, 14 15, 16. Oct. 1, 2, 3, 4, 5, 6.	June 4, 5, 6, 7, 8, 9. Aug. 13, 14, 15, 16, 17, 18. Sept. 17, 18, 19, 20, 21, 22.

COMPLIMENTS AND BEST WISHES OF

HARRY C. McALLISTER

CANDIDATE FOR SHERIFF

VOTING NUMBER 117, MARK X

Harry McAllister sought the Republican Party nomination for sheriff of Multnomah County in 1912 and used the popularity of the Portland Beavers baseball team to promote his candidacy. Both had a bad year. McAllister lost, and the Beavers did not win the pennant. Dave Bancroft (bottom row, second from right) is a member of the National Baseball Hall of Fame.

The productive results of a hard-fought season are found in this pair of postcards. The *Oregonian* published the image without the pennant in March 1912 with the caption, "The Monroe High School baseball team has been putting in some strenuous practice in preparation for the season of 1912. The boys have splendid grounds, good material and a capable manager and leader. They hope to arrange for games with other teams in the state." Their efforts paid off: they were undefeated and won the Benton County School League title, as celebrated in the other postcard with the "Monroe High School Champions of 1912" banner. The team played in a league with Bellfountain High School, Alsea High School, and Philomath College.[102]

O.A.C. Rooter Section   O.A.C. vs. U. of O.

"Brownie has on the striped uniform," wrote shortstop Lester Hutt on a 1912 postcard he sent home showing him tagging third baseman Brownie Groce, his teammate at Oregon Agricultural College. From the same year comes a postcard (top) of the rooter section at the November 23, 1912, Civil War contest held in Albany and won 3–0 by the University of Oregon.[103] Note the formal attire worn by those who attended.

PORT ORFORD VS GOLD BEACH
JULY 4 1912

The baseball game postcard shows a July 4, 1912, contest between Port Orford and Gold Beach in Curry County. The message on the postcard of the 1912 Norway team from nearby Coos County states, "This is the bunch that goes South today to teach Curry Co. the game. We have only lost one game this year and that to the Myrtle Point League team." Myrtle Point was in a league that year with North Bend, Coquille, Marshfield, Bandon, and Eastside (an area in the eastern part of what was then Marshfield).[104]

These undated postcards show Portland's Palace Laundry team and the Lents Giants baseball club. In 1913, Palace Laundry won the Laundry League championship, while Beaverton defeated Lents in the title contest of Portland's Archer and Wiggins League (named for a sporting goods store of the same name). The Palace and Lents teams met in March 1914, with Lents winning 23 to 3. Perhaps the Palace Laundry team sensed before the contest that they were in trouble—that morning the following notice ran in the *Oregonian*: "Fast amateur catcher wanted. Apply Palace Laundry today, 9:30 a.m."[105]

BASKET BALL FLORENCE VS MAPLETON   FLORENCE 42.

145 lb. STATE CHAMPIONS.

The postcard of an outdoor women's basketball game between Florence and Mapleton High Schools likely depicts one of three contests between the schools during the Rhododendron Carnival in Florence on May 28 and 29, 1913. Florence won the series 2–1. The other postcard is captioned "145 lb State Champions" and shows the 1912–1913 Mt. Angel College basketball team after they beat Portland's Jewish Boys' Athletic Club 20–19 to win the title.[106]

October 15, 1913.

Dear Friend:

Following is the schedule of Portland Academy Football Games for 1913.

HILL MILITARY ACADEMY, October **17.**
LINCOLN HIGH SCHOOL, October **29.**
JEFFERSON HIGH SCHOOL, November **7.**
WASHINGTON HIGH SCHOOL, November **19.**

We have not lost a game yet this year. Come and enjoy yourself and see P. A. win. All games played at Multnomah Field.

JAMES F. EWING,
Assistant Principal

RALPH J. HURLBURT,
Coach and President Alumni Association

Portland Academy, PORTLAND, Oregon.

Football player, coach, and Portland attorney Ralph J. "Spec" Hurlburt, whose name appears as coach on the 1913 postcard encouraging attendance at Portland Academy games, was killed during World War I at age twenty-nine, on September 29, 1918. Hurlburt had an illustrious football life. He played at the Portland Academy, then with the University of Michigan in 1909 and 1910 (he graduated with a law degree), and in 1912 he was selected as the Multnomah Amateur Athletic Club's team captain. He coached the Portland Academy team from 1912–1914, and later officiated games.[107] The 1910-era postcard of the Portland Academy shows baseball players on the diamond and gathered by the school.

During a world tour promoting baseball, the Chicago White Sox and New York Giants played a November 1913 game in Medford, as advertised on the postcard. Fans paid two dollars for tickets and watched the Giants win 3–0 in five innings in a rain so steady that Giants outfielder Sherry Magee made a one-handed catch while holding an umbrella over his head. Two years later, major leaguers from the American and National Leagues on a post-season barnstorming trip played in Pendleton. Hall of Famer Johnny Evers of the Boston Braves is shown there in November 1915, flanked on one side by Amos Strunk of the Philadelphia Athletics and on the other by a Native American on horseback. The "Nationals" won 7–3 over the "Americans."[108]

ROSEBURG OUTLAWS 1913

Miss Fay Hill, "Queen of the Moose," was transported on a decorated float on Moose Day (named for the fraternal organization) during Roseburg's fifth annual Strawberry Festival and Rose Show, held from May 21–24, 1913. The festival was intended to advertise the Umpqua Valley. There were bands, parades, balloon rides, a strawberry luncheon, a barbecue, cowboy exhibition, and a baby competition in which "Beauty counted for nothing in this contest, the awards being based entirely on the physical structure of the entrant." At the festival, the Roseburg Outlaws baseball team in the postcard played the University of Oregon, Oregon Agricultural College, and Oakland (Oregon).

The postcard on the right likely shows Myrtle Creek players warming up before a game at Roseburg in that era.

The camaraderie of sports shines through in these baseball postcards of a 1918–1919 trio of Oregon Agricultural College players captioned "The Village Ruffnecks, OAC Rooks" and a pair of Roseburg players in 1913.

The image in this postcard appeared in the *Oregonian* in July 1913 with this explanation: "The Newberg High School baseball team has played twelve games this season and has won ten of them. The state championship for high schools stands a tie between Jefferson High of Portland, Salem, and Newberg." Newberg had already won the crowns of Polk, Yamhill, and Washington Counties, so with state honors still up for grabs, the trophy at their feet likely celebrated one of those recent titles. Ultimately, the state championship went to Salem.[110]

A dramatic 1913 postcard of a horse race looks so perilous that finishing first likely came second to finishing at all. "The way we do it in Union, Oregon" is written on the front.

The "NAC" on the jerseys of the team in a 1913 baseball postcard is likely short for Nehalem Athletic Club. The other postcard is of the Nehalem Camp Tigers, a team felled from a logging camp. It likely dates to 1918 when press coverage of the team appears.[111]

YELLOW JACKETS BASKET BALL TEAM, SALEM, OREGON.

The YMCA's Salem Yellow Jackets was one of the first basketball teams in its area to organize for the 1913–1914 season. There was a swarm of activity when the Yellow Jackets buzzed to Silverton for their opening game against the Silverton Commercial Club. A special train, a brass band, and 125 rooters accompanied them in a veritable hive of excitement. The Yellow Jackets went down to a stinging defeat. Their next game was a one-point loss to Mt. Angel that afterward had the Yellow Jackets hissing: the referee had been Mt. Angel's coach.[112]

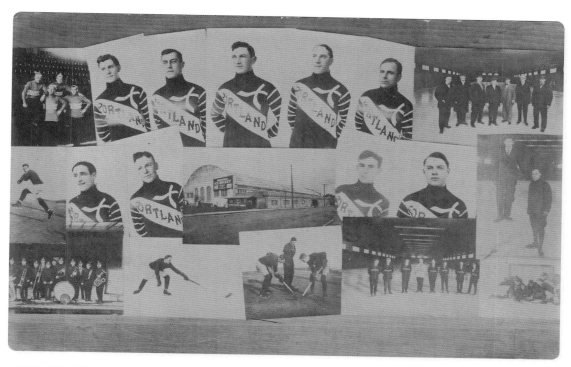

In 1916, the Portland Rosebuds became the first American hockey team to play for the Stanley Cup, losing to the Montreal Canadiens. The Rosebuds, also called the Portland Uncle Sams, played in the Pacific Coast Hockey Association. The top postcard portrays the 1914–1915 team. Hockey Hall of Famer Moose Johnson is in the top row, fourth portrait from the left. The other postcard shows their arena, the Portland Ice Hippodrome at NW Twenty-First and Marshall. A billboard advertises their 1915–1916 home opener in which Portland defeated Vancouver 2–1.[113]

This photo of the 1914 University of Oregon football team includes coach Hugo Bezdek (top row, second from left), the only person to manage a major league baseball team (Pittsburgh Pirates, part of 1917–1919) and coach in the National Football League (Cleveland Rams, 1937 and part of 1938). He coached Oregon's football team in 1906, and from 1913 through 1917, when in his final year he led the team to its first Rose Bowl win.[114] Its second came in 2012. Standing at the far right is Bill Hayward, the University of Oregon's athletic trainer and track coach.

HUBBARD GIANTS BASE BALL CLUB

H. L. HUBBARD, MGR.   BOX 745   PORTLAND, OREGON

CHAMPION COLORED TEAM OF THE PACIFIC NORTHWEST.

Southpaw pitcher Jimmy Claxton became the first African American to play organized baseball in the twentieth century when he pitched for the Pacific Coast League's Oakland Oaks on May 28, 1916.[115] That same year he became the first black player to appear on an American baseball card (with the Oaks). He kneels in the front row, far right of the bottom postcard of Portland's 1914 Hubbard Giants baseball team, named for its manager Lew Hubbard. He played for them in 1915, as well. The top postcard presents the team in about 1911 when they were known as the Portland Giants.

Newberg High School's basketball team is shown in a postcard returning home from a road win over Forest Grove High in January 1914. They recorded their victory on the basketball and their suitcases: "On my way to Newberg" next to a drawing of a goat is written on one; "We Are It" on another; and on a third, "39 to 15 Newberg!!" They were at that time on the cusp of a state championship, but then they dropped two games to McMinnville by a total of three points, allowing McMinnville to assert claim to the title.[116]

WILLAMETTE FOOTBALL SQUAD 1915.

Salem High School marked its home win over Eugene High School in November 1914 with this postcard—note the inscription over the football: "Salem 26 Eugene 0." At halftime the fans of each team formed two lines on the field and shook hands with the person opposite them. We can all be grateful that never caught on. Willamette University's 1915 team in the other postcard won four of six games and claimed to have earned the non-conference state title.[117]

George "Admiral" Dewey wears Oregon Agricultural College track garb in a circa 1915 postcard. At OAC he played quarterback for the football team, was an all-northwest guard on the basketball team, and was successful in track. After college, he became a coach at several Portland high schools, including Franklin and Lincoln. At Franklin, he coached the football, basketball, and track teams for three seasons, including in 1917 when the football team was not scored on and won the interscholastic league title. At Lincoln, he coached the basketball team to a state championship in 1918.[118]

Race cars tear down the track at the Portland's Rose City Speedway, circa 1915.

Images of female athletes during the early twentieth century are scarcer than those of their male counterparts. Women wearing bloomers play baseball on the University of Oregon campus in a circa 1915–1920 photo. A postcard from that same period captures women running hurdles at Oregon Agricultural College in front of the Alpha Chi Omega sorority house—the current site of Johnson Hall—perhaps at a Field Day.

Football powerhouse Reed College was feared throughout the land for its Aristotle defensive alignment and the Herodotus slant play, both developed there when this photo was taken in 1915. None of this is betrayed by the mild note on the postcard's reverse, "Scene during the football game. You can see the dormitory in the distance." Reed's linebackers pause dramatically in the set position, ready to engage in critical thinking. The school's tradition of using discarded copies of Aristophanes' *The Clouds* in lieu of pads began in this era. (This is satire, of course. Reed is known for many things. Football is not one of them.)

The 1912-era photo of Reed on the right was taken from near SE Woodstock and Cesar Chavez Boulevard.

CHICAGO AMERICAN GIANTS
April 1, 1915 — Portland, Ore.

The African American baseball team Chicago American Giants stands in front of Portland's Golden West Hotel in this postcard taken on April 1, 1915. Their game scheduled for that day at Vaughn Street Park against an all-star team from Portland's City League was rained out. The Giants played in the west that spring; their games included a 7–3 loss to the Portland Beavers in Fresno, California, on March 21, 1915, while Portland trained there. Three of the Giants—Pete Hill (fifth from left, jacket over arm), Louis Santop (tall player in doorway) and Rube Foster (fifth from right in light attire)—are in the Hall of Fame. In 1914, thirty-three years before Jackie Robinson integrated major league baseball, Beavers manager Walter McCredie bluntly declared, "I don't think the color of the skin ought to be a barrier in baseball."[119]

A 1915 postcard of the Arlington baseball grounds depicts rural Oregon baseball. Railroad tracks run between a church rising in the distance and the game in the foreground. "Arlington Diamond" appears on the negative, and the postcard bears an August postmark; perhaps this game was held during Independence Day celebrations. The *Oregonian* announced that "Arlington will celebrate Independence Day on July 2 and 3. Friday will be given over to social get-together times, with the first ball game between Arlington and Olex in the afternoon. On Saturday the usual parade, speaking, broncho-busting and more ball games will be held."[120] The other postcard depicts the Olex team from around that time.

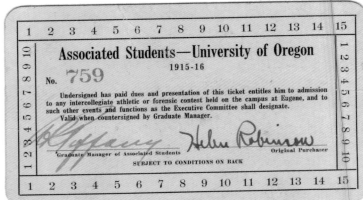

"Oregon Is Winner in Sea of Mud, 9–0" was the *Oregonian*'s headline summary for the 1915 Civil War football game played in Eugene. The poster stamp and pin promoted that contest. The unused 1915–1916 ticket would have admitted its holder to the game, but the conditions that day were reason enough to stay home. The weather: "frigid, wind and rain-swept." The field: "Kincaid field was a mire. No sewer digger ever had to toil under more unfavorable conditions. Real football was out of the question. Water stood around on the surface in small lakes. Forward passing and good kicking was impossible."[121]

The Eastern and Central Oregon champion Prineville team, likely the one in this undated postcard, faced off against West Portland's Baby Beavers, the 1916 Inter-City Baseball League winner, at the Crook County Fair. Their four-game series was Oregon's first statewide semipro championship. The Baby Beavers, whose roster included ex-major leaguers Howie Haworth and Carl Druhot, won four straight games and took home Oregon's semipro title.[124]

"Columbia Club Champions, Lower Columbia River 1916," reads the caption to this postcard of Astoria's football team. "By winning, 3 to 0, from the West Astoria football team on Thanksgiving day, the Columbia Club eleven, of this city, won the undisputed championship of the Lower Columbia for the 1916 season. Leo Larson, former Oregon Agricultural College athlete, won the Turkey-day game with his thirty-five-yard dropkick. The Columbia Club eleven finished the year without being scored on," the *Oregonian* reported. A dropkick, a rarity today, occurs when a player drops the ball and kicks it after it touches the ground. The hero of the game, Larson, stands in the top row at the far right.[125]

Johnny Gamble, a University of Oregon freshman in 1918, lettered in baseball and in basketball. He wore this uniform and glove as a member of the baseball team. Adding a touch of mystery to the attire is that the uniform appears to be from the 1918 varsity team, and research reveals no record of Gamble having played varsity baseball until 1919. [126]

Commercial League Champions 1918.

The Capital National Bank was the undefeated champion of the Salem YMCA's Commercial Basketball League in 1918. The league, which was in its fourth year, had four teams. The "money changers" (as the newspaper called them) were 10–0 that year, with each of the other entries suffering three losses.[127] Their jerseys bear the initials "CNB."

A prohibition of alcoholic beverages began in Oregon in 1916 and nationally in 1920; both ended in 1933. The National Prohibition Campaign sign in this postcard advocates their ban during World War I as the first step toward a prohibition of alcohol in the federal constitution, later fulfilled by the 18th Amendment. The "Feb. 9, Sat. night" note written in chalk corresponds to the 1918 calendar. A game—likely basketball—between the "girls" of Silverton and Hubbard is written next to that date. The athlete appears to be wearing basketball attire.

A-150   EUGENE GAME 11-15-19.

The first game played at Hayward Field in Eugene, named for the University of Oregon's famed trainer Bill Hayward, was a Civil War contest on November 15, 1919. Fittingly, UO won in a 9–0 shutout of Oregon Agricultural College.[128] The image in the postcard was taken during the game and looks onto the end bleachers under the west goal. In the lower left is a circle drawn around a fan, presumably a prior owner of the postcard who attended the game. Hayward Field remains in use today.

Coach Harold Quigley Chauncey Hightman; Ray Weston ; Clarence Walker; Clarence King.

Jess Dyman; Morgan Staton; Arthur Sutton; Clarence Ekstrom; Tim Colvin; Reginald Towsey; Harlan Gram; dad Lively; Glen Hurt; Ken Julian; Louis Coulter; Norman Youmans.

JEFFERSON HIGH SCHOOL TEAM

Championship Interscholastic League. · 1919 ·

Jos. E. Weiser
J.H.S. Williamette

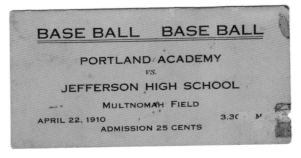

BASE BALL BASE BALL

PORTLAND ACADEMY
VS.
JEFFERSON HIGH SCHOOL

MULTNOMAH FIELD

APRIL 22, 1910   3.30 M
ADMISSION 25 CENTS

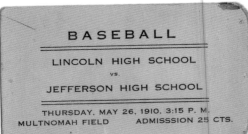

BASEBALL

LINCOLN HIGH SCHOOL
VS.
JEFFERSON HIGH SCHOOL

THURSDAY, MAY 26, 1910, 3:15 P. M.
MULTNOMAH FIELD   ADMISSSION 25 CTS.

The 1919 Jefferson High School team in the photo won the Interscholastic Football League title with an 8–0 record. The two Jefferson High School baseball tickets correspond with notable events. The April 22, 1910, ticket was for Jefferson's first game in its first year of baseball in the Portland Interscholastic. Jefferson beat 7–2 Portland Academy. The May 26, 1910, ticket was for Jefferson's last game of that initial season, an 8–1 win over Lincoln High School. The win gave Jefferson the Columbia Hardware Company silver trophy cup for second place in the league. The *Oregonian* observed: "This game closed a most successful season in the Interscholastic League. This was Jefferson's first year in the league and second place over teams like Columbia University, Lincoln High School and Portland Academy is indeed an honor."[129]

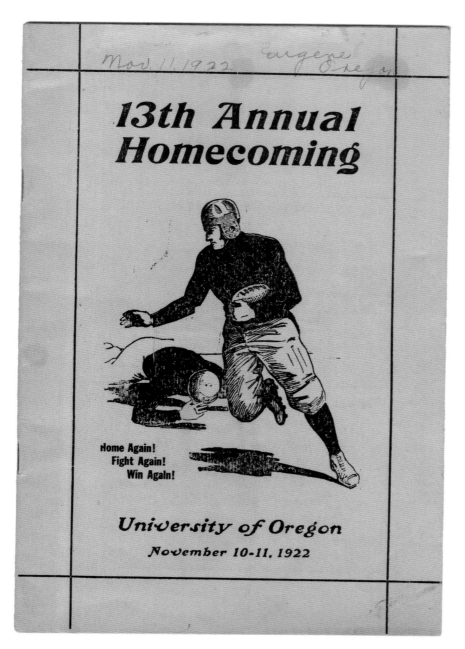

13th Annual Homecoming

Home Again!
Fight Again!
Win Again!

University of Oregon

November 10-11, 1922

Twelve thousand fans of the lemon yellow saw the Washington State Cougars threaten Oregon's goal just once in their 13–0 loss to the Webfooters at Hayward Field in 1922. Two UO touchdowns and a missed extra point on a wet field explain the score. "You Can't Beat Oregon Fight," reads a green-lettered banner at the rear of the bleachers. Unfortunately, the Oregon fans went slightly nutty before the game: "The university men, impatient for things to begin and pepped up to see the teams in action, got unruly beyond the control of the yell leaders and commenced to hurl peanuts and other missiles at passersby."[130]

This final photo captures why we relate to sports. The runner on first hopes to advance. The first baseman anticipates a double play. The catcher signals for a high and tight pitch. The pitcher stretches in mid-delivery. The batter coils for a swing. The umpire stands motionless behind the pitcher, poised to make a call. The fans pause in anticipation. This moment before they burst into action—one repeated in every sporting event and in everyday life—is frozen in time. No one on the field knows what will come next, but there they are, alone and together, ready to try their best.

Portland 1910-era baseball postcard, location unknown,
by photographer A.C. Weber

NOTES

BASEBALL

1   "Base Ball," *Oregonian*, May 30, 1866, City; "Portland Had Champion Nine in Early Days," *Oregonian*, July 12, 1903, Section Three. This article includes the names of those involved at each step of the club's organization, as drawn from the record books of player and team manager Joseph Buchtel.

2   The Pioneer Base Ball Club's date of organization is June 2, 1866. "Portland Associations and Societies," *Oregonian*, January 10, 1867, City; "Base Ball," *Oregonian*, June 5, 1866, City; "Portland Had Champion Nine in Early Days," *Oregonian*, July 12, 1903, Section Three; F. L. McCormick, *Portland Directory for 1880*, 8 (population); "Baseball in Portland Forty Years Ago," *Oregonian*, November 8, 1903, Section Three (lists twenty-nine names who signed the constitution); "Portland Had Champion Nine in Early Days," *Oregonian*, July 12, 1903, Section Three (the thirty-one signatories of the club's constitution came from club's record book belonging to player and manager Joseph Buchtel and is presumed to be accurate); S. J. McCormick, *Portland Directory for the Year Commencing January 1866,* Business Directory, 87–99, 105 (Portland businesses).

3   "Sports in Pioneer Days," *Oregonian*, October 14, 1900, Section Three. For base: "The sides were chosen as described. The bases were about one hundred yards apart. One side would send one of their men out who would go as near as he dared to the other base without being caught. If he was touched by any member of the opposite side he had to go and play on that side. If a boy from one side could run around the other base without being touched he had a right to choose two players from the opposite side. Thus, you see, the best runners and the best dodgers were always in demand." For three-cornered cat: "The choosing of partners would be the same as described. There were three bases in the shape of a triangle and a boy on each base with a catcher behind him. If the striker missed the ball and the catcher caught it either on the fly or on the first bound he was entitled to strike. The boy who was caught out would have to catch. Every time a striker hit the ball they all had to run to the next base. If the ball was caught or was thrown in front of one while he was running he was out."

4   "Original Fan Medford Man," *Medford Mail Tribune*, August 1, 1910.

5   "Do You Remember," *Oregonian*, July 9, 1922, Section Two.

6   "Match Game," *Oregonian*, October 15, 1866; "Organizations on the Ball Field," *New York Clipper*, October 27, 1866; 1867 Pioneer Base Ball Club circular, Oregon Historical Society (reference Belknap 1043a) and is quoted in full in note 45 on page 206.

7   "Pioneer Ball Club," *Oregonian*, July 28, 1866, City; "Base Ball", *Oregonian*, July 28, 1866, City.

8   Paul Dickson, *The Dickson Baseball Dictionary*, 3rd ed. (New York: W.W. Norton & Co., 2009), 391 ("grounds"); "Base Ball," *Oregonian*, June

30, 1866, City (the article mentions a Pioneers game to be played on Monday, July 2, 1866, and also refers generally to prior games they had played); "Base Ball," *Oregonian*, July 28, 1866, City ("The young men composing the Pioneer Base Ball Club have taken a new field for their sports on Oak street, in the vicinity of Fifth and Sixth streets. . . ."); "Do You Remember," *Oregonian*, July 9, 1922, Section Two (The Pioneer club "played between 1866 and 1869 on the grounds now bounded by Fifth and Sixth and Oak and Stark streets, and later on Raleigh's field, a ten-acre lot, on part of which now stands the Oregon and Benson hotels and other buildings."); "Base Ball," *Oregonian*, September 8, 1866, City; "Base Ball," *Oregonian*, August 31, 1866, City.

9   "Do You Remember," *Oregonian*, July 9, 1922, Section Two; "Base Ball Players," *Oregonian*, June 18, 1867, City (club initials on jerseys); "Base Ball," *Oregonian*, May 28, 1873 (uniform); "Base Ball," *Oregonian*, May 28, 1873 (black cap and belt).

10   "Portland's First Ball Team Played at Broadway and Stark 50 Years Ago," *Oregon Daily Journal*, April 20, 1913.

11   "Portland's First Ball Team Played at Broadway and Stark 50 Years Ago," *Oregon Daily Journal*, April 20, 1913; "Do You Remember," *Oregonian*, July 9, 1922, Section Two; *Pacific Base-Ball Guide for 1867* (San Francisco: A. Roman & Co., 1867), 2.

12   "Base Ball," *Oregonian*, July 28, 1866, City; "Match Game of Base Ball," *Oregonian*, August 3, 1866, City; "Base Ball," *Oregonian*, August 4, 1866, City; (No headline), *Oregonian*, August 3, 1866, New Today; "Match Game of Base Ball," *Oregonian*, August 3, 1866, City.

13   Paul Dickson, *The Dickson Baseball Dictionary*, 3rd ed. (New York: W. W. Norton & Co., 2009); "Match Game of Base Ball," *Oregonian*, August 3, 1866, City.

14   "Organizations on the Ball Field," *New York Clipper*, October 27, 1866. Dickson, *The Dickson Baseball Dictionary*, 667.

15   "Base Ball," *Oregonian*, August 31, 1866, City; "Off Again," *Oregonian*, September 4, 1866, City; "Pioneer Base Ball Club," *Oregonian*, September 26, 1866, City (meeting for the purpose of electing the first nine to occur that night); "Portland Had Champion Nine in Early Days," *Oregonian*, July 12, 1903, Section Three (team's executive committee recommended the first nine on October 2, 1866); "Pioneers," *Oregonian*, September 28, 1866, City (game between the first nine and club members); "Portland's First Ball Team Played at Broadway and Stark 50 Years Ago," *Oregon Daily Journal*, April 20, 1913; Dickson, *The Dickson Baseball Dictionary*, 325, 756.

16   "The Base Ball Game," *Oregonian*, September 1, 1866, City; Base Ball, *Oregonian*, September 24, 1866, City.

17   "A Challenge," *Oregonian*, October 5, 1866, City; "A Match Game," *Oregonian*, October 6, 1866, City; "Base Ball," *Oregonian*, October 8, 1866, City (roster); "The Pioneers," *Oregonian*, October 10, 1866, City (itinerary).

18   "Match Game," *Oregonian*, October 15, 1866, City; John Freyer and Mark Rucker, *Peverelly's National Game* (San Francisco: Arcadia Publishing, 2005) 115.

19   "Match Game," *Oregonian*, October 15, 1866, City.

20   "Base Ball Player's Convention," *New York Clipper*, December 22, 1866, Ball Play; "The Appointment of the Committees," *New York Clipper*, December 29, 1866, Ball Play; "Return Game," *Oregonian*, November 2, 1866, City (Robert H. Law chosen as delegate); "The Pioneer Base Ball Club," *Oregonian*, March 29, 1867, City. "Important to Base Ball Clubs and Players," *New York Clipper*, November 24, 1866, Ball Play. In 1866 the New York City Base Ball Emporium advertised for sale in the *New York Clipper* baseball photographs and cards of teams. They invited teams from across the United States to send in team photos, along with a description of the uniform the club wore, for the "First Annual Exhibition of Pictures

of Base Ball Players." The exhibition was to be held in New York on December 14, 1866, two days after the convention. It is unclear whether the exhibition occurred.

21 "Return Game," *Oregonian*, November 2, 1866, City; "Where is the Pioneer Club?" *Oregonian*, March 28, 1867, City.

22 "Another Base Ball Club," *Oregonian*, April 24, 1867, City; "New Base Ball Club," *Oregonian*, May 15, 1867, City. The *Oregonian* (May 18, 1867) announced their formation as the Wide Awake Base Ball Club. (No headline), *Oregon Sentinel*, May 11, 1867 (dateline May 7).

23 "A New B.B. Club to be Organized," *Oregonian*, July 31, 1867, City; "Serious Accident," *Oregonian*, May 21, 1867, City.

24 "Base Ball," *Oregon City Enterprise*, March 23, 1867, Town and County.

25 "Dissolved," *Oregon City Enterprise*, November 24, 1866, Town and County; "Base Ball," *Oregon City Enterprise*, March 30, 1867, Town and County; "State Items," *Oregonian*, May 29, 1867; (No headline), *Oregonian,* June 19, 1867, State Items; "Letters from the Interior of the State," *Oregonian,* July 25, 1867 (dateline July 22, 1867).

26 "The Match Ball Game," *Oregonian*, June 18, 1867, City; "Base Ball Match," *Oregonian*, July 6, 1867, City; "Challenge," *Oregonian*, September 7, 1867, City. The challenge text: "Challenge! AT A REGULAR MEETING OF THE PIONEER BASE BALL CLUB held Sept. 2d, 1867, the following resolution was adopted. *Resolved*, That this Club is prepared to receive a challenge from any Club in this State or Washington Territory, to a match game of Base Ball, to be played at Salem during the coming State Fair (Oct. 7th to 12th). Challenges will be received up to the 25th September. G.A. STEEL, Sec'y."

27 "Base Ball," *Oregonian*, September 16, 1867, City. For a report on the supposed acceptance of the challenge by the Clackamas club, *see* "Base Ball Challenge Accepted," *Oregon City Enterprise*, September 14, 1867.

28 "The Pioneer's Matches," *Oregonian*, September 28, 1867, City; "Pioneers vs. Willamettes", *Oregonian*, October 11, 1867, City; "The State Fair," *Oregonian*, October 10, 1867 (dateline October 8, 1867) (setting prize); "Pioneers vs. Clackamas Club,: *Oregonian*, October 12, 1867, City ("The result of this game gives the Pioneers the champion $40 bat offered by the State Agricultural Society"); "Pioneer vs. Clackamas Club," *Oregon City Enterprise*, October 19, 1867, Town and County (box score); "The State Fair," *Oregonian*, October 14, 1867 (dateline October 11, 1867).

29 (No headline), *Oregonian*, November 30, 1867, New To-day.

30 "Do You Remember," *Oregonian*, July 9, 1922, Section Two; Buchtel's gallery was also a team gathering place—see "Pioneer Base Ball Club," *Oregonian*, April 15, 1867, City ("Members will meet at the Photograph Gallery of Jos. Buchtel this (Monday) evening at seven o'clock for the purpose of reorganizing for the season of 1867"); "Fine Work," *Oregonian*, September 30, 1868, City; "That Premium Bat," *Oregonian*, June 19, 1868, City. The bat, which was purchased in California, was presented to the Pioneers in a ceremony in front of Portland's Cosmopolitan Hotel on September 19, 1868—see "Presentation," *Oregonian*, September 19, 1868, City; "Premium Bat," *Oregonian*, September 21, 1868, City; (No headline), *Oregon City Enterprise*, September 26, 1868, Farm Items (quoting remarks made at the ceremony).

31 "Uniform Caps for Pioneer B.B. Club," *Oregonian*, August 23, 1867, City.

32 "Base Ball," *Oregonian*, May 30, 1866, City; "Letters from the Interior of the State," *Oregonian,* July 25, 1867 (dateline July 22, 1867); "The Great Topic," *Oregonian*, July 25, 1867, City.

33 "Base Ball," *Oregon State Journal*, June 22, 1867; "Base Ball," *Oregon State Journal*, July 13, 1867 (for the officers elected to the club, see "Base Ball," *Oregon State Journal*, July 20,

1867); "Base Ball Match," *Oregon State Journal*, August 10, 1867.

34 "Pole Raising," *Oregon City Enterprise*, June 29, 1867, Town and County.

35 "Portland Slightly Ahead," *Oregonian*, October 10, 1867, City; "Base Ball," *State Rights Democrat*, June 27, 1868.

36 "Lost Once," *Oregonian*, August 24, 1868, City.

37 "Attention Club!" *Oregonian*, July 1, 1867, City.

38 "Attention Club," *Oregonian*, July 2, 1867, City.

39 "Base Ball Players," *Oregonian*, June 18, 1867, City; "Portland's First Ball Team Played at Broadway and Stark 50 Years Ago," *Oregon Daily Journal*, April 20, 1913; "Baseball in Portland Forty Years Ago," *Oregonian*, November 8, 1903, Section Three.

40 "Base Ball on the Ice," *Oregonian*, January 13, 1868, City; "From Oregon City," *Oregonian*, January 18, 1868, City.

41 "Base Ball Guide," *Oregon City Enterprise*, May 4, 1867, Town and County; "Acknowledgement," *Oregonian*, April 19, 1867, City (stating that Mr. F. Roman had brought *The Pacific Base Ball Guide* to the *Oregonian*); "Base Ball Caps," *Oregon City Enterprise*, August 3, 1867; (No headline), *Oregonian*, May 19, 1868, New To-Day; (No headline), *Oregonian*, June 12, 1871, New To-day.

42 "Vancouver Items," *Oregonian*, May 25, 1867, City; "Vancouver Items," *Oregonian*, February 23, 1867, City (The *Oregonian* had reported on February 9, 1867, that a base ball club there was about to organize); "The 'First Nine,'" *Oregonian*, May 28, 1867, City; "Base Ball," *Oregon City Enterprise*, June 1, 1867, Town and County.

43 "What a Comparison," *Oregonian*, May 29, 1867, City.

44 "Vancouver Items," *Oregonian*, June 11, 1867, City; "Vancouver Items," *Oregonian*, August 31, 1867 City (the Sherman Club is "principally composed of soldiers stationed at this post"); "The Game at Vancouver," *Oregonian*, September 5, 1867, City, (Continental); "Washingtons vs. Occidentals," *Oregonian*, October 26, 1867, City, (Washington);

"Vancouver Items," *Oregonian*, June 27, 1868, City; "Orientals vs. Washingtons," *Oregonian*, September 4, 1868, City (Oriental); "Boys in Blue vs. Washingtons," *Oregonian*, July 23, 1868, City, (Boys in Blue); "Pioneers Still Alive," *Oregonian*, July 29, 1868, City (Young Washingtons).

45 "Base Ball Matters," *Oregonian*, February 15, 1868, City; "Oregon City Items," *Oregonian*, October 28, 1867, City. The circular is headed "Pioneer Base Ball Club, Portland, Oregon, Oct. 1st, 1867," is addressed, "To the [blank space] Base Ball Club," and reads as follows: "Gentlemen—In this country within the past ten years the game of Base Ball has assumed a position of so much importance that it is universally acknowledged to be THE game of America; and it being emphatically an American game, you, no less than ourselves, desire that it shall ever maintain that position of dignity and importance already attained, and to which it is so justly entitled; and in order that our State may have State representation in the National Association of Base Ball Players, and believing it to be generally desired by the several Clubs of the State that there be a general organization for the purpose of fostering the interests of the game, and whereby unanimity as to rules and regulations may be arrived at, therefore, the Pioneer Base Ball Club of Portland, by virtue of being the pioneer Base Ball Club of Oregon, does, by this letter, request your Club to designate two persons, as delegates, who, together with a like number from each of the several Clubs throughout the State, will meet in convention in the city of Portland, on Friday, the 21st day of February, 1868, for the purpose of organizing an Association of Base Ball Players for the State of Oregon. Your approval, co-operation and an early reply are cordially solicited. We have the honor to remain, Gentlemen, Very respectfully, your obd't serv'ts," followed by spaces for signatures from the team President and Secretary. The document is located at the Oregon Historical Society (reference Belknap 1043a).

46　"Oregon City Items," *Oregonian*, October 28, 1867, City. Similarly, the *Oregonian* stated on January 30, 1868, "We have been requested to call the attention of the several Base Ball clubs of the State to the circular issued some months ago by the Pioneer club of this city, inviting all the clubs of the State to meet them by delegates in a State convention, to be held in Portland on the 21st day of February, proximo. The design of the convention is to organize a State Association of Base Ball players. Thus far, we believe but few of the clubs have responded to the invitation; but there is yet time to elect delegates, and it is desired that *all* the clubs of the State take such action." ("Base Ball Convention," *Oregonian*, January 30, 1868, City.)

47　"Base Ball Convention," *Oregonian*, February 22, 1868, City.

48　"Base Ball," *Oregonian*, September 26, 1868. The announcement, which was repeated two days later, stated the meeting would be held on the first Tuesday in October 1868, which corresponds to October 6, but the meeting actually occurred on Saturday, October 10, per a subsequent press report ("Proceedings of the B. B. Association," *Oregonian*, October 12, 1868, City).

49　"Proceedings of the B.B. Association," *Oregonian*, October 12, 1868, City. Although it is not known what clubs joined the association, other Oregon baseball clubs that were formed by the end of 1868 were from Albany (Web-foot), Oregon City (Young Grant), Portland (Union), and a team from an unknown location called Academic. The Albany team may have been formed in 1867 as the *Oregonian*, June 4, 1867, State Items, p. 2, stated that the "Journal" (likely the *Albany Journal*) said an Albany team "will be formed." For the Web-foot Club, see "Base Ball," *State Rights Democrat*, June 27, 1868. For the Young Grant club, see "Base Ball," *Oregonian*, July 13, 1868, From the North, and on the same page for the Union club, see the article headed "B.B." For the Academic club, see "Match Game," *Oregonian*, November 2, 1868,

City. The Tigers from Forest Grove played the Academic team there, so perhaps the Academic team was from in or near Forest Grove.

50　Proceedings of the B.B. Association, *Oregonian*, October 12, 1868, City. Given the context, a "junior club" may have referred to one not in the association. A more precise definition is, "A club in the early days of baseball made up of players under the age of 18." Dickson, Paul, *The Dickson Baseball Dictionary*, 3d ed. W.W. Norton & Co., 2009, 475.

51　"Portland Had Champion Nine in Early Days," *Oregonian*, July 12, 1903, Section Three; "Centennial Celebration," *Oregonian*, July 8, 1876.

52　"Four-Team League Formed," *Oregonian*, March 12, 1910 (in the league were Stanfield, Hermiston, Echo, and Umatilla); "Schedule of Games Blue Mountain League," *East Oregonian*, March 14, 1910 (in the league were Weston, Athena, Pendleton, and Pilot Rock); "Oh! You Fan, Paste This in Your Hat", *Medford Mail Tribune*, March 24, 1910 (in the league were Medford, Grants Pass, Central Point, and Jacksonville); "Salem Wins Cup in Tri-City Play," *Oregonian*, August 29, 1910 (in the league were East Portland's Dilworth Derbies, West Portland's Rupert's Rubes, Sellwood, Salem, Vancouver, and Peninsula. During the season the original Vancouver club was replaced by the First Infantry team of Vancouver Barracks, and the Peninsula team was replaced by Portland's Fulton Blues club. Both replacement teams retained the names of the teams they stepped in for.); "Standing in Hardware League," *Oregonian*, May 9, 1910, (in the Columbia Hardware League were Gill Butchers, Pop Corn Kings, Calef Brothers, Robinson & Co., Peninsula, Albina Cubs, Meier & Frank, Arleta, Red Front, Sellwood, Newsboys, and Midway); "Albany in League", *Oregonian*, February 26, 1910, (in the league were Albany, Eugene, Springfield, and Cottage Grove).

53　Portland had teams in the Pacific Northwest League of 1890, 1891, 1892; 1893 Oregon

State League; 1896 New Pacific League; and Northwest League of 1901 and 1902.

54 "Oaks Baseball Park," *Oregonian*, August 7, 1885, New To-day.

55 "New Baseball Park," *Oregonian*, August 7, 1885, Local and General (the Oaks); "Baseball!" *Oregonian*, May 1, 1885, New To-Day (City View Park; steamer and barge to leave from the foot of Salmon Street, "No disreputable characters admitted"); "Base Ball Grounds," *Oregonian*, April 11, 1888, The East Side (Clinton & McCoy location); "Base Ball," *Oregonian*, July 22, 1888, (for a game at the Clinton & McCoy grounds, "A Boat and Barge from Washington street, the Bridge Railway and Jefferson street ferry afford quick and cheap transportation"); "Open-Air Concert Tonight," *Oregonian*, Coming Attractions, July 4, 1893 (West End ball grounds location and grandstand capacity); "Used the New Ranges," *Oregonian*, July 22, 1901 (West End ball grounds location); "Vicissitudes of Portland Baseball Recalled by Opening of New Park," *Oregonian*, April 21, 1912 (summary of early baseball grounds).

56 "Amateur Athletics," *Oregonian*, June 14, 1914, Section Two; "Amateur Athletics," *Oregonian*, May 16, 1915, Section Two; "Negro Teams Wins at St. Paul," *Oregonian*, June 14, 1915, "Amateur Athletics," *Oregonian*, June 20, 1915, Section Two; "Colored Giants Beat Barton," *Oregonian*, July 26, 1915.

FOOTBALL

1 *Portland City Directory, 1890* (Portland, OR: R.L. Polk & Co.), 42 (population); "Won By a Score of 8 to 0," *Oregonian*, November 28, 1890.

2 Tom Benjey, *Spalding's Football Guides for 1883, 1888, 1889, 1890, 1891, and 1893* (Carlile, PA: Tuxedo Press, 2011), 103–110 (1890 rules).

3 "Won By a Score of 8 to 0," *Oregonian*, November 28, 1890 (Bishop Scott); "Gregory's Sport Gossip," *Oregonian*, February 22, 1930, Section Two (Gavin); "In Fields of Sport," *Oregonian*, October 24, 1892; "Foot Ball in the Northwest," *Oregonian*, November 19, 1899;

"Gregory's Sport Gossip," *Oregonian*, February 22, 1930, Section Two; A. Powers and H. M. Corning (editors), *History of Education in Portland* (Portland: State System of Higher Education, 1937), 202, http://library.state. or.us/repository/2015/201501071025503 /part2.pdf; "Rules for 'Prep' Athletes Scored," *Oregonian*, March 23, 1913, Section Two; "Do You Remember?" *Oregonian*, February 26, 1922, Section Two.

4 "Will Organize a Football Club," *Oregonian*, August 28, 1890, Specific Information; "Football Club Organized," *Oregonian*, August 31, 1890, Rounds of the City; "A Second Meeting Held," *Oregonian*, September 4, 1890; "Prospective Football," *Oregonian*, September 10, 1890; "Foot Ball in the Northwest," *Oregonian*, November 19, 1899 (football before 1890 meant rugby); for examples of association games in both sports, see "Football Matters," *Oregonian*, September 23, 1890, News in Sideheads (preference for rugby); "The Footballers Have Rare Sport," *Oregonian*, October 13, 1890; "An Exciting Game of Football," *Oregonian*, October 27, 1890; "Football Today," *Oregonian*, November 2, 1890, Items Around Town.

5 "Kick It High, Boys!" *Oregonian*, September 17, 1890 (transition to athletic club); *Biennial Report of the Secretary of State of the State of Oregon* (Salem: State of Oregon, 1891), 140, https://play.google.com/books/read-er?id=Azg4AAAAMAAJ&printsec=frontcov-er&output=reader&hl=en&pg=GBS.PA140 (incorporating the PAAC); "Thanksgiving Sport," *Oregonian*, November 26, 1890; "Today's Football Game," *Oregonian*, November 27, 1890 (lineups for the soccer game); "Football for Thanksgiving," *Oregonian*, November 5, 1890, The Sidehead Column. Getting the new P.A.A. Club name slightly wrong, the *Oregonian* reported November 5 that the "Portland Amateur Athletic Association" would meet to select a team for a Thanksgiving Day "football match," but did not specify the sport. This may have

referred to soccer, for that sport is known around the world as football.

6   "When First Played in Portland," *Oregonian*, November 23, 1902, Section Four; "Big Turkey Day Game is Historic," *Oregonian*, November 24, 1912, Section Two (Note that the former article says the P.A.A.C's coach in the game, Will Lipman, went to Princeton; the latter says Harvard); "Won By a Score of 8 to 0," *Oregonian*, November 28, 1890.

7   "Amateur Athletic Club," *Oregonian*, January 25, 1891, In the Local Field; "To Promote Healthy Exercise," *Oregonian*, January 30, 1891; "Meeting Notices," *Oregonian*, February 14, 1891; "The Boys Mean Business," *Oregonian*, February 18, 1891; "The P.A.A. Club," *Oregonian*, February 22, 1891, News of a Busy City (seeking location that will be filled with modern gym equipment and facilities); "Meeting Not Harmonious," *Oregonian*, February 28, 1891, In the Sporting World; *Biennial Report of the Secretary of State of the State of Oregon*, (Salem: State of Oregon, 1893), 164 (recorded as the "Multnomah Amateur Club"), https://play.google.com/books/reader?id=yDhKAQAAMAAJ&printsec=frontcover&output=reader&hl=en&pg=GBS.PA164; "Portland Amateur Athletics," *Oregonian*, March 12, 1891 (club name changed to "Multnomah Amateur Athletic Club").

8   "Its Success Assured," *Oregonian*, March 24, 1891; "The Boys Mean Business," *Oregonian*, February 18, 1891 (PAAC committee members); "Incorporated," *Evening Capital Journal*, March 2, 1891 (filing of Multnomah Club Articles of Incorporation and list of signatories); "The M.A.A. Club," *Oregonian*, March 4, 1891, Sports of All Kinds (identifying M.A.A.C. Board of Trustees and officers).

9   "Foot Ball in the Northwest," *Oregonian*, November 19, 1899 ("Portland Football Club"); "When First Played in Portland," *Oregonian*, November 23, 1902, Section Four ("Portland Football and Cricket Club"); "Chapin Its Head," *Oregonian*, February 26, 1905, Section Two ("Portland Football, Cricket and Athletic Club"); "Big Turkey Day Game is Historic," *Oregonian*, November 24, 1912, Section Two (same); "Know Your City and State," *Oregonian*, November 3, 1927 ("Portland Football and Athletic Club").

10   "New Football Team Organized," *Oregonian*, September 29, 1891, City News in Brief; "Football at the Oaks," *Oregonian*, November 1, 1891 (the article states that the score was 8–0, but on November 2, 1891, the *Oregonian* published a correction. "The Football Game," *Oregonian*, November 2, 1891, Other Sporting News.)

11   "Vicissitudes of Portland Baseball Recalled by Opening of New Park," *Oregonian*, April 21, 1912, Section Two (identifying location of The Oaks as the corner of SE Morrison and First); "Know Your City and State," *Oregonian*, November 3, 1927 (identifying location of The Oaks as E Second between Morrison and Belmont); "Our New Ball Park," *Oregonian*, March 16, 1891 (describing The Oaks as follows: "These grounds are located alongside of the East Side Southern Pacific railway track, and a short distance south of N street"—in current directions, between SE First and Second Avenues and Belmont and Morrison); "Football Gossip," *Oregonian*, November 15, 1891, All Kinds of Sports; "Football at the Oaks," *Oregonian*, November 22, 1891; "Other Kinds of Sports," *Oregonian*, November 23, 1891, General Sporting News.

12   "Football at the Oaks," *Oregonian*, November 22, 1891; "Portland 30, Tacoma 6," *The Seattle Post-Intelligencer*, November 27, 1891.

13   "Tacoma Did Not Score," *Oregonian*, January 2, 1892; "Chapin Its Head," *Oregonian*, February 26, 1905, Section Two.

14   "Preparing for a Football Game," *Oregonian*, December 3, 1892, Other Kinds of Sport; "A Battle of Giants," *Oregonian*, January 3, 1893; "Portland's Enthusiasts Accompany the Multnomah Team to Seattle," *Oregonian*, January 2, 1893, Today's Football Game.

15   "Football Game at Forest Grove," *Oregonian*, November 11, 1892, Other Kinds of Sport

(Bishop Scott preparing for game); "Football at Forest Grove," *Oregonian*, November 13, 1892, College Football (results); "Football is the Raging Fad," *Oregonian*, November 14, 1892, In Fields of Sport (recap); (No headline), *West Side*, November 10, 1893; "The Game at Forest Grove," *Oregonian*, November 5, 1893, Game of Football ("The first regular intercollegiate game of football was played between the Monmouth state normal school and the Pacific university. The game resulted in a score of 54 to 0 in favor of the Pacific university.")

16 Foot Ball," *The Corvallis Gazette*, November 10, 1893; "A Game at Corvallis," *Oregonian*, November 12, 1893 (game recap and attendance); "Foot Ball," *The Corvallis Gazette*, November 10, 1893 (admission cost).

17 "Academy Football," *Oregonian*, January 23, 1893; "High School Juniors," *Oregonian*, November 26, 1893; "Willamette Notes," *Capital Journal*, November 4, 1893.

18 *Daily Eugene Guard*, October 31, 1893; *Daily Eugene Guard*, November 7, 1893.

19 *Daily Eugene Guard*, March 23, 1894.

20 "Gregory's Sport Gossip," *Oregonian*, February 22, 1930, Section Two.

21 "Football in Eugene", *Oregonian*, March 25, 1894, All Around Oregon; "Foot Ball," *The Eugene City Guard*, March 24, 1894 (citing the *Eugene Daily Guard*, dateline March 21, 1894)

22 "Corvallis vs. Eugene," *Oregonian*, November 4, 1894; (No headline), *Oregonian*, December 31, 1894, Great Week of Sport; *Corvallis Gazette*, October 19, 1894, Newsy College Notes. Willamette University applied to the association too late to enter its team. Portland University won the title with a 4–0 record, followed by Oregon Agricultural College (3–1), Pacific University (1–2–1), the University of Oregon (1–2–1), and Oregon State Normal School (0–4

23 "Pedal Spheroid," *The Corvallis Gazette*, September 26, 1895; "Corvallis Failed to Score," *Oregonian*, October 27, 1895.

24 *Hillsboro Independent*, October 26, 1894 (Pacific College vs. Pacific University); "OAC

Championship," *Oregon Union*, November 26, 1897; "Corvallis Team Won," *Oregonian*, December 5, 1897.

25 "Football Cruelty Will be Modified," *Oregonian*, March 27, 1910.

26 "What Will the New American Football Be?" *Oregonian*, September 23, 1906, Section Three; "Football Rules Greatly Changed," *Oregonian*, August 18, 1910; "Football Rules Have Changes," *East Oregonian*, October 2, 1912.

27 "No One Knows What Kind of Game to Expect," *Oregonian*, September 23, 1906, Section Three.

28 "Multnomah Beats Albany 34 to 0," *Oregonian*, October 21, 1906, Section Two; "Agrics Cannot Score at Seattle," *Oregonian*, October 28, 1906; "Seattle Loses to Multnomah," *Oregonian*, December 26, 1906.

29 "Critics Picking 'U' Men to Beat Club," *Oregonian*, November 23, 1913, Section Two.

30 "Numbers Are Success," *Oregonian*, November 28, 1913.

BASKETBALL

1 "YMCA Athletics," *Evening Capital Journal*, January 16, 1893; "Mount Hood," *Hood River Glacier*, February 23, 1905; "Ione," *Gazette-Times*, October 3, 1912; "High School Notes," *St. Johns Review*, January 24, 1919.

2 "For Men and Women," *The Dalles Daily Chronicle*, June 20, 1893.

3 "For Men and Women," *The Dalles Daily Chronicle*, June 20, 1893.

4 *Daily Morning Astorian*, December 16, 1893, About the City.

5 "At the Gymnasium," *Daily Morning Astorian*, January 28, 1894, About the City.

6 "Basket Ball Team," *State Rights Democrat*, December 14, 1894, Thursday; "Indoor Athletics," *Daily Morning Astorian*, March 14, 1894; "University Exercises," *Capital Journal*, June 20, 1895.

7 "Basket-Ball Introduced," *Oregonian*, March 16, 1895, City News In Brief.

8 "Conference Ended," *Oregonian*, April 29, 1895 ("lively game"); "More Basket Ball," *Oregonian*, May 14, 1895 (nine-on-nine); "At

the YMCA," *Oregonian*, July 25, 1895 ("principal amusement").

9   "More Basket Ball," *Oregonian*, May 14, 1895.

10   *Daily Eugene Guard*, February 20, 1895, University Notes; *Daily Eugene Guard*, February 14, 1895, University Notes (freshmen women versus sophomores); "Basket Ball," *Daily Eugene Guard*, February 16, 1895 (same); *Daily Eugene Guard*, February 23, 1895, University Notes ("The juniors and seniors are now drilling for the coming basket ball contest between the two teams"—presumably a reference to women's teams as reported on in those earlier articles); *Oregonian*, June 23, 1895, East Side Affairs (west and east YMCA game).

11   "Society in Bloomers," *Oregonian*, December 22, 1895.

12   "A Class in Physical Training," *The Dalles Weekly Chronicle*, September 21, 1895.

13   "Basket Ball," *Daily Capital Journal*, April 27, 1897 (Willamette vs. Chemawa); *Oregon Mist*, November 26, 1897, Clatskanie Notes (Merrill); "Basket-Ball Game," *Daily Capital Journal*, April 29, 1898 and *Oregonian*, April 30, 1898, Capital Notes (OAC vs. Chemawa).

14   "Basket Ball Tonight," *La Grande Evening Observer*, December 2, 1905, Sports.

15   "Spalding's Athletic Library," *Oregon Courier*, March 6, 1896; "Holiday Goods," *Oregonian*, December 15, 1901, Section Three; "Pig Skins," *Roseburg Plaindealer*, October 27, 1902; *Oregonian*, December 20, 1908, Section Three ("Honeyman Hardware").

16   "Greg's Gossip," *Oregonian*, October 19, 1969, Sports; "1908–09 Cagers were first of 'trail blazers,'" *Oregonian*, July 10, 1977, Sports. The October 19, 1969, *Oregonian* article includes a list of their games and scores which, when tabulated, reveals that they won 49 games, lost eight, and tied one, playing in 19 states (one state is not identified, but the game was against the Haskell Indians, a Kansas team).

17   "OAC Quintet Victorious," *Oregonian*, January 17, 1909, Section Two; "Oregon Steamrollers Buckeye Five 46 to 33 to Take National Title," *Oregonian*, March 28, 1939.

18   "Basketball's Birthday," *Oregonian*, January 21, 1917, Section Two, Personal Touches in Sport.

OTHER SPORTS

1   "Jolly Skaters," *Daily Morning Astorian*, December 1, 1896; "Montreal Team is Hockey Champion," *Oregonian*, March 31, 1916.

2   "International Cricket Match," *Oregonian*, July 9, 1878; *Daily Morning Astorian*, September 20, 1885 (lacrosse); *Eugene City Guard*, April 3, 1886, City and County (polo); *Daily Morning Astorian*, July 7, 1896, Around Town (golf).

3   "A New Play-thing," *Oregonian*, August 14, 1866, City.

PHOTO GALLERY

1   The Pioneer club's constitution was likely signed in June 1866 when it was officially organized. Wiley was a signatory ("Portland Had Champion Nine in Early Days," *Oregonian*, July 12, 1903, Section Three). While this image could be from 1866, it is assigned a circa 1867 date because in that year he was identified in the press as a Pioneers player ("The Athletics Against the Eclipses," *Oregonian*, August 5, 1867, City; "Base Ball," *Oregonian*, New To-day, August 23, 1867; "Pioneer vs. Clackamas Club," *Oregon City Enterprise*, October 19, 1867, Town and County); "Death of Captain Joseph R. Wiley," *Oregonian*, February 9, 1894; The 1867 *Pacific Coast Business Directory* lists twenty-two photographers around Oregon (compare 1867 *Pacific Coast Business Directory*, 527 and appendix).

2   "Joseph Buchtel, Pioneer, Is Dead," *Oregonian*, August 11, 1916.

3   *State Rights Democrat*, April 11, 1873.

4   *Eugene City Guard*, January 5, 1884.

5   "Yesterday's Contests," *Daily Morning Astorian*, June 12, 1885.

6   *Oregon, Washington and Idaho Gazetteer*, 1886–87, 154 (listing S. B. Graham at the corner of 3d and L—since renamed Washington St.—in east Portland).

7   "Base Ball," *Evening Capital Journal*, July 21, 1890; "Misfits," *State Rights Democrat*, July 25, 1890.

8   *The Dalles Times-Mountaineer*, August 15, 1891; Paul Dickson, *The Dickson Baseball Dictionary*, 3rd ed. (New York: W. W. Norton & Co., 2009).

9   Moore was working out of the 29 Washington address on the photo mount in 1891 (*Oregon, Washington and Idaho Gazetteer*, 1891–92, p. 483) and the Portland Rowing Club was organized in 1891, so it's likely also the date of the photo. "Portland Rowing Club," *Oregonian*, April 7, 1891; "Life on the Wave," *Oregonian*, May 4, 1891; "The Portland Rowing Association," *Oregonian*, May 6, 1879, City. The Portland Rowing Association was organized on May 3, 1879.

10 "Will Have a Housewarming," *Oregonian*, December 6, 1893, City News In Brief; *Oregonian*, December 10, 1893, Other Events.

11 "Twenty-Five Years' Career of Multnomah A.A. Club Reviewed," *Oregon Journal*, April 30, 1916, Section Three.

12 *Albany Daily Democrat*, March 1, 1894, Home and Abroad; *Daily Eugene City Guard*, March 20, 1894; "Foot Ball," *The Eugene City Guard*, March 24, 1894 (citing the *Eugene Daily Guard*, dateline March 21, 1894).

13 "Agricultural College Notes," *The Dalles Daily Chronicle*, May 17, 1894.

14 "Glen Quits Oregon," *Oregonian*, July 26, 1911. Although the article calls him the father of Oregon intercollegiate athletics, the university's first football game in 1894 preceded the baseball contest. The article also mis-states the score for that first baseball game. The correct score was 32–23 in favor of the Corvallis team.

15 "They Play Today," *Oregonian*, February 24, 1894 (ticket); "Who is Champion?" *Oregonian*, February 25, 1894; "Claim of Corvallis," *Oregonian*, February 27, 1894 (for more about the disputed championship in 1894).

16 "Co. G Won the Trophy," *Oregonian*, April 16, 1891; "Know Your City and State," *Oregonian*, November 3, 1927; "Baseball," *Oregonian*, June 6, 1891, City News in Brief; "Pieces of Pastime," *Oregonian*, June 7, 1891.

17 Two articles read together clarify the location of The Oaks between SE First and Second Avenues and Belmont and Morrison: "Vicissitudes of Portland Baseball Recalled by Opening of New Park," *Oregonian*, April 21, 1912, Section Two (at the corner of SE Morrison and First); "Know Your City and State," *Oregonian*, November 3, 1927 (on E Second between Morrison and Belmont); "Our New Ball Park," *Oregonian*, March 16, 1891 (special box for the Multnomah Amateur Athletic Club in the grandstand).

18 *Oregonian*, May 19, 1893.

19 "Easy for Stanford," *Oregonian*, July 19, 1894.

20 "Eugene Wins, 6 to 4," *Oregonian*, November 17, 1895.

21 "Corvallis Was Shut Out," *Oregonian*, December 11, 1898.

22 McMillan played football for Stanford from 1893 to 1894, for Oakland's Reliance Athletic Club in 1895, and for Montana's Butte team in 1896 and Anaconda in 1897. "Chosen as Stanford Football Coach," *Oregonian*, April 30, 1901; "George M'Millan Returns," *Oregonian*, November 14, 1901 (Stanford coach); "Football Player for President," *Oregon Daily Journal*, February 7, 1907 (McMillan had variously been manager, coach, and captain of the football team); "Club Loses Last Game of Season," *Oregonian*, January 2, 1909 (McMillan "wound up his 11th year today as a member of the club eleven"); "Train Ends Life," *Oregonian*, April 8, 1911; "G.W. M'Millan Killed By Train," *Oregonian*, April 8, 1911; "Football Player for President," *Oregon Daily Journal*, February 7, 1907.

23 "Chosen as Stanford Football Coach," *Oregonian*, April 30, 1901.

24 "Death of O. P. Lent, Pioneer of 1852," *Oregonian*, April 23, 1899.

25 "Champions of Inter-scholastic League and Winners of Feldenheimer Trophy," *Oregonian*, June 10, 1900, Section Three (the article includes this same photo with player identifications); "Academy's Closing Will Cause Regret," *Oregonian*, March 12, 1916.

26 "Personal and Local," *Oregon Mist*, July 10, 1896 ("A match game of baseball is expected to take place between the St. Helens and Clatskanie nines in the near future.")

27 "Klepper to Buy M'Credie's Club," *Oregonian*, October 23, 1921, Section Two; "Portland Team Sold to Turner," *Oregonian*, October 22, 1924; "Portland Baseball Club Changes Hands," *Oregonian*, September 27, 1942, Section Five; "Fans to Honor Pennant Winners with 'Owen Day,'" *Oregonian*, September 18, 1945, Section Two.

28 "Academy Boys Won," *Oregonian*, October 31, 1901.

29 "Wm. Beck & Son," *Eugene City Guard*, May 29, 1880; "Oregon Champions at Tennis Hopeful," *Oregonian*, July 2, 1922, Section Two; "Tennis Rackets Restrung," *Oregonian*, May 16, 1912.

30 "May Day Picnic," *Weekly Coast Mail*, April 30, 1904.

31 "Clubmen Defeat Soldiers," *Oregonian*, May 16, 1904 (Astoria Commercial Club); "Three Days' Sports," *Oregonian*, May 19, 1904 (Puget Sound coast artillery); "Cathlamet's Fifth Victory," *Oregonian*, June 6, 1904). Years later, on June 21, 1942, a Japanese submarine I-25 destroyed the backstop of the Fort Stevens baseball field.

32 "Houlton Joins St. Helens," *Oregonian*, November 16, 1913.

33 "Greg's Gossip," *Oregonian*, August 18, 1955, Section Two; "Corvallis Varsity Beats the Alumni," *Oregon Daily Journal*, October 1, 1905. For more coverage, see "OAC Bests Alumni," *Oregonian*, October, 1, 1905, Section Two; "Wins First Game," *Corvallis Gazette*, October 3, 1905; "Alumni Scored," *The Corvallis Times*, October 4, 1905.

34 "Entry List for Big Indoor Meet," *Oregonian*, March 3, 1906; "Games to Aid Athletes," *Oregonian*, March 2, 1906; "Portland Most Generous of All Contributors," *Oregon Daily Journal*, April 12, 1906; "Benefit is Success," *Oregonian*, March 4, 1906, Section Two; "Third Place for High Jump," *East Oregonian*, May 1, 1906.

35 "Giants Take the First Game, 1–0," *Oregonian*, April 8, 1906, Section Two; "Now Own the Team," *Oregonian*, December 4, 1904, Section Two; "Ely Sells Interest," *Oregonian*, December 17, 1905, Section Two.

36 "Cards Stacked, M'Credie Says," *Oregonian*, November 6, 1917; "Portland Colts Offered for Sale," *Oregonian*, December 21, 1912 (identifying W. W. McCredie as president and owner of the Colts).

37 "Company F Winner," *Oregonian*, May 22, 1906; "Company F Men Win Finals," *Oregon Daily Journal*, May 22, 1906.

38 "Basketball Season Ends," *Oregonian*, March 18, 1907; *Oregon Daily Journal*, February 12, 1907 (for this same photo with player identifications); "OAC Claims Championship," *Oregonian*, March 17, 1907, Section Four; "Defeats Old Willamette," *Oregonian*, February 23, 1907; "Pennant is Safe," *Polk County Observer*, February 26, 1907.

39 *Oregon Daily Journal*, March 5, 1907, Sporting Gossip of the Day (Chicago Crescents); "OAC Claims Championship," *Oregonian*, March 17, 1907, Section Four; Oregon Agricultural College yearbook, *The Orange*, 1908, unnumbered page headed, "OAC First Team Basketball."

40 For a different photo of the 1907 Oregon Agricultural College women's team and their identities, see "OAC Girls' Basketball Team," *Oregon Daily Journal*, January 20, 1907; "Local and Personal," *Corvallis Gazette*, April 5, 1907.

41 "Oregon Wins Game," *Oregonian*, October 21, 1906.

42 *Evening Herald*, February 29, 1908, Merrill Record Items.

43 "1913 Bowling Record Broken," *Oregonian*, August 13, 1913.

44 "Issues a Football Number," *Oregonian*, December 22, 1907, Section Two (scores for 1907 season); "Champions of Pacific Coast," *Oregonian*, November 29, 1907; "Champions of the Coast" (same); "Oregon Has Two Champion Teams," *Oregonian*, December 1, 1907, Section Four.

45 "Canby," *Oregon City Courier*, April 19, 1907; "Canby Baseball Team Has Record of Winning The Longest Shut-Out Game This Season," *Oregonian*, July 31, 1907. The latter article includes this same photo with player identifications.

46 "Sodaville Gets High School," *Oregonian*, March 21, 1909 ("The college gave up its work a year ago").

47 "Albany Seeks Another Game," *Oregonian*, November 16, 1908.

48 "Oregon Defeats Idaho 27 to 21," *Oregonian*, November 1, 1908, Section Two; "Great Gridiron Games Promised," *Oregonian*, July 19, 1908, Section Four; "Washington Won Highest Honors," *Oregonian*, December 6, 1908, Section Four.

49 "Oregon Triumphs in Great Game," *Oregonian*, November 22, 1908.

50 "Results of Each Event," *Oregonian*, July 26, 1908; *Oregonian*, September 12, 1908 and September 13, 1908 (Boye postal cards).

51 "Games Postponed," *La Grande Evening Observer*, April 22, 1908; "City Vacated Durinc [sic] Game," *La Grande Evening Observer*, April 29, 1908 (games played the following week); "Inland Empire Baseball Flag is La Garnde's [sic]," *La Grande Evening Observer*, July 11, 1908. For the final standings, see "Standing of the Clubs," *La Grande Evening Observer*, July 13, 1908.

52 "Pitcher Wins Coquille Girl," *Coos Bay Times*, September 8, 1908; "Bandon Wins Close Game," *Coos Bay Times*, August 24, 1908 (includes league standings).

53 "Elgin Banquets 'Cy' Young," *Oregonian*, February 18, 1910.

54 "Dallas Basket Ball Team to Advertise Oregon in East," *Oregonian*, December 12, 1908 (article included photo with player identifications); "Dallas Boys Win Again," *Oregonian*, December 20, 1908, Section Two (55–14 win over Spokane on December 19); "Greg's Gossip," *Oregonian*, October 19, 1969, Sports; "1908–09 Cagers were first of 'trail blazers,'" *Oregonian*, July 10, 1977, Sports. The October 19 *Oregonian* article includes a list of their games and scores which,

when tabulated, reveals that they won forty-nine games, lost eight, tied one, and played in nineteen states (one state is unidentified, but the game was against the Haskell Indians, a Kansas team).

55 "OAC Wins Over Whitman," *Oregonian*, February 28, 1909; "Oregon Agricultural Defeats Whitman," *East Oregonian*, March 12, 1909; "OAC Quintet Victorious," *Oregonian*, January 17, 1909, Section Two.

56 For portraits of the 1908 Woodburn Blue Birds, see "Woodburn Baseball Team, Leaders of the Tri-City League," *Oregon Journal*, July 26, 1908, Section Five; "Girls to Play Baseball," *Oregonian*, June 16, 1909 (Scio).

57 "Boys' Rules Girls' Desire," *Oregonian*, November 19, 1909.

58 "A Base Ball Match," *Eugene City Guard*, October 25, 1879.

59 "Prineville Wins Baseball Series," *Crook County Journal*, June 3, 1909.

60 A similar, but not identical, image appears with players identified in "Members of Baseball Team at Banks," *Oregonian*, May 9, 1909.

61 *Oregonian*, June 6, 1873, Base Ball.

62 "Hudson Arms is Loser," *Oregonian*, July 17, 1911.

63 "Play Tie-Game," *Coos Bay Times*, April 26, 1909; *Coos Bay Times*, April 27, 1909; "Says Game Was Tie," *Coos Bay Times*, April 30, 1909; "Wet Weather Didn't Hurt Cooston Fourth," *Coos Bay Times*, July 8, 1909.

64 "Baseball Team at Hubbard," *Oregonian*, June 20, 1909, Section Three. The *Oregonian* article included this same photo with player identifications.

65 "Grocers to Frolic," *Oregonian*, July 18, 1909; "Picnic Big Success," *Oregonian*, July 23, 1909. The *Oregonian* published photographs of the Camas team (identifying players) standing in front of this same scoreboard on August 7, 1909 ("Team Goes Thus Far in Season Without Suffering Defeat") and June 13, 1910 ("Fast Camas Amateur Nine Has Unbroken Record of Victories"). The players standing (not kneeling) by the scoreboard probably

include Camas (fifth from left), Portland's Honeyman Hardware (first from left and, based on the hat, fourth from left), L. S. Frakes, and Behnke Walker. For a 1909 photograph of the Honeyman Hardware indoor team wearing the identical uniforms to the one in the postcard, see "Honeyman Hardware Company Indoor Baseball Team, One of Leaders in City League Pennant Race," *Oregonian*, December 19, 1909, Section Two.

66 "Baseball," *The Daily Capital Journal*, July 2, 1908, City News ("The state house stars will meet the penitentiary guards tonight in the first baseball game between the two teams"); "Chemawa Beats Penitentiary," *Oregonian*, July 3, 1910, Section Two; "What Willamette is Doing," *Daily Capital Journal*, April 15, 1911, Section Two.

67 "Baseball Tournament Planned," *Times-Herald*, July 24, 1909;

68 "Suits for Corvallis Nine," *Oregonian*, June 22, 1909; "Go To Monroe Next Saturday," *Corvallis Daily Gazette*, May 18, 1909; "Talk of the Town," *Corvallis Daily Gazette*, May 26, 1909; "Corvallis a Winner," *Daily Gazette-Times*, September 9, 1909.

69 "University Men Rally for Fray," *Oregonian*, November 19, 1909; "Oregon Wins In Brilliant Game," *Oregonian*, November 20, 1909.

70 "Husky Football Squad at University of Oregon from Which Coach Forbes Sent Two Complete Elevens against Multnomah Yesterday," *Oregonian*, November 7, 1909, Section Four (article includes player identifications); "Yale Eleven is Victorious," *Oregon Daily Journal*, November 25, 1906, Sports; "Better Teamwork Wins for Oregon," *Oregonian*, November 14, 1909, Section Four.

71 "Eugene High School Football Team Aspires to State Championship," *Oregonian*, October 21, 1909 (article includes player identifications); "Freshmen Defeat Eugene," *Oregonian*, October 17, 1909; "Eugene High After Laurels," *Oregonian*, November 25, 1909; "Eugene High Beats Salem," *Oregonian*, November 26, 1909; "Willamette Valley Schools Quarrel Over

Honors," *East Oregonian*, November 30, 1909 (state title).

72 "M'Credie's Team Ready for Battle," *Oregonian*, March 16, 1909.

73 "Beavers Run Away With White Sox 2," *Oregonian*, March 17, 1909.

74 "M'Credie Off for East; Team North," *Oregonian*, November 8, 1910.

75 "Fred Brown Will Handle the Astoria Browns," *Oregon Daily Journal*, February 24, 1907.

76 "Athletics," *Weekly Chemawa American*, November 22, 1907 (two players named Lafky in the lineup). See also, e.g., "Columbia Defeated Salem High," *Daily Capital Journal*, November 19, 1910; "Salem High Play Against Washington," *Daily Capital Journal*, November 3, 1911.

77 "Exponents of Yesterday's Soccer Game, in which Multnomah Wins, 3 to 0," *Oregonian*, December 26, 1909, Section Four (the team photo in this article includes some of the players on the postcard, which helped identify them as the Cricketers); "Multnomah Wins Champion's Prize," *Oregonian*, March 6, 1910, Section Two.

78 Richard L. Forstall, compiler and editor, *Oregon Population of Counties by Decennial Census: 1900 to 1990* (Washington, DC: US Bureau of the Census, 1995), https://www.census.gov/population/cencounts/or190090.txt (1910 population of 20,309); "Four-Team League Formed," *Oregonian*, March 12, 1910 (Stanfield, Hermiston, Echo, and Umatilla); "Hermiston Ball Boys Banqueted," *East Oregonian*, July 21, 1910; "Schedule of Games Blue Mountain League," *East Oregonian*, March 14, 1910 (Weston, Athena, Pendleton, Pilot Rock); "Weston Refuses to Play Pendleton," *East Oregonian*, July 2, 1910 "Blue Mountain League Schedule," *East Oregonian*, March 7, 1911 (Weston, Athena, Pendleton, Echo, Milton-Freewater, Walla Walla); "Buckarooes Trim Pennant Winners," *East Oregonian*, July 3, 1911; "Adams Boys Bat Out a Victory," *East Oregonian*, May 3, 1910; "Personal Mention About Adams People," *East Oregonian*, June 10,

1911; "Alba and Ukiah Play Ball Sunday," *East Oregonian*, June 22, 1911.

79   "Mt. Angel Trip," *Weekly Chemawa American*, June 17, 1910.

80   "People Here and There," *East Oregonian*, April 23, 1920.

81   "Newly-Elected Baseball Captain of the Behnke-Walker Business College," *Oregonian*, February 27, 1910, Section Three; "Behnke-Walker Business College Team," *Oregonian*, May 8, 1910, Section Two (includes same photo and identifies players); "New League is Formed," *Oregonian*, April 12, 1911.

82   The *Oregonian* published this same photo with player identifications. See "OAC Wrestlers, in Defeating University of Washington Grapplers, Become Northwest Champions," *Oregonian*, April 12, 1910.

83   "Southern Oregon Town Has Baseball Team That Stands at Head of Willamette League," *Oregonian*, May 21, 1910 (article identifies players); "Nesmith Selected as Name of Proposed New County," *Oregonian*, January 11, 1909; "Nesmith County," *Medford Mail Tribune*, March 23, 1910; "Albany High School Basketball Team Scores Total of 554 Points, to 364 for Opponents," *Oregonian*, March 28, 1910 (identifying an Albany High School opponent as "Nesmith team of Cottage Grove"). "Cottage Grove Defeats Varsity," *Oregonian*, June 1, 1909.

84   "Valley Ball League Planned," *Oregonian*, January 31, 1910; *Daily Capital Journal*, February 24, 1910 ("The Nesmith Baseball Association has secured new grounds for the coming season, and will enclose them and erect a grand stand as soon as the weather will permit").

85   "Machine Rises from Ground," *Oregonian*, June 9, 1910, City News in Brief.

86   "OAC Pins Faith to Track Team Captain to Win at Portland Meet," *Oregonian*, April 16, 1910; "University Team Wins Track Meet," *Oregonian*, April 17, 1910, Section Two.

87   "Pennant Hangs on Corvallis' Walls," *Oregonian*, June 5, 1910, Section Two.

88   "Marshfield 1910 Champs," *Coos Bay Times*, November 14, 1910.

89   Meier & Frank advertisement, *Oregonian*, May 8, 1909.

90   "Today Opens Cricket Season," *Oregonian*, April 16, 1910; Portland Cricket Club Faces Great Season," *Oregon Journal*, April 2, 1911, Section Four (for the same photo with players identified).

91   "Cricket," *Oregon City Enterprise*, July 6, 1867 ("At the conclusion of the base ball games on Thursday, in this city, the bats, wickets and ball for a genuine old-fashioned game of Cricket were brought out. The play attracted great attention"); *Oregonian*, July 7, 1873, Local Brevities "Cricket Club," *Oregonian*, July 8, 1873, City; "The New Cricket Club," *Oregonian*, July 17, 1873, City "Out Door Sports," *Oregonian*, July 26, 1873.

92   "Corvallis Loses to Albany," *Oregonian*, April 15, 1911.

93   "Falls City Organizes Baseball Team for 1911," *Oregonian*, March 22, 1911. The newspaper's caption to the team photo includes player identifications.

94   "Cornelius Cubs Win the Pennant," *Hillsboro Argus*, August 17, 1911.

95   "Big Events Slated," *Oregonian*, July 3, 1911; "Chautauqua Open, Thousands Attend," *Oregonian*, July 5, 1911; "Chautauqua Has Its Banner Crowd," *Oregon City Enterprise*, July 7, 1911.

96   "Mystery No More," *Oregonian*, July 2, 1911, Section Two; "New Coach is Due," *Oregonian*, March 25, 1911. This same photo along with a biography appears in the Oregon Agricultural College yearbook, The Orange, 1913, 289.

97   "High School Commencement," *Times Herald*, May 13, 1911.

98   *Oregon Journal*, March 24, 1912, Amateur Athletics.

99   "Crack Knights of Columbus Baseball Team Which Is Planning Strong Lineup for Next Year," *Oregonian*, November 3, 1912, Section Two; "Knights of Columbus Baseball Team Had Good Record," *Oregon Journal*, November 3, 1912, Section Three; "City News," *Daily Capital Journal*, May 2, 1913; "Portland Team is

Winner of Game," *Daily Capital Journal*, May 5, 1913; "Portland Team is Winner of Game," *Daily Capital Journal*, May 5, 1913.

100 "In Brilliant Game Aggies Lose, 9 to 3," *Oregonian*, November 10, 1912.

101 "Weed Team Now Champions," *Oregonian*, July 6, 1912.

102 "Monroe High School Baseball Team Expects Busy Season," *Oregonian*, March 28, 1912 (in one version of this *Oregonian* page, this photo is included and players identified); "Monroe Wins Championship," *Oregonian*, May 17, 1912.

103 "Field Goal Gives Oregon 3; OAC 0," *Oregonian*, November 24, 1912.

104 "Standing of Clubs," *Coos Bay Times*, July 27, 1912.

105 "Palace Team is Champion," *Oregonian*, August 7, 1913; "Won the Cup," *The Owl*, October 18, 1913; "Amateur Athletics," *Oregonian*, March 23, 1914; *Oregonian*, March 22, 1914, Section Two.

106 "Florence Carnival is Biggest Success Yet," *Oregonian*, June 2, 1913 ("As the first game of the series had been a victory for Florence and the second a tie, the score of 14 to 10 in favor of the Florence school gave them the pennant for the season"); "Mt. Angel Quint Wins," *Oregonian*, March 13, 1913; "Mount Angel College Junior Basketball Team Claims 145-pound Title of Northwest," *Oregonian*, March 30, 1913, Section Two (article includes this same photo with players identified).

107 "Death Report Confirmed," *Oregonian*, November 27, 1918 (for a photo of the 1913 Portland Academy team with Hurlburt that identifies players, see "Coach Ralph 'Spec' Hurlburt and his Portland Academy Eleven Which Held the Heavy Lincoln High Team to a 12–0 Score Last Wednesday," *Oregonian*, November 2, 1913, Section Two); "Hurlburt is Captain," *Oregonian*, September 14, 1912; "New Captain of Multnomah Club Football Eleven," *Oregonian*, September 15, 1912, Section Two; "Ralph Hurlburt Engaged to Wed," *Oregonian*, April 23, 1913; "Convill Stars 12 Years on Gridiron," *Oregonian*, January 11, 1914, Section Two (list of captains). "Portland Schools Show Big Increase,"

Oregonian, September 17, 1912; "California Reply Awaited," *Oregonian*, June 21, 1915.

108 "Giants Shut Out White Sox, 3 to 0," *Oregonian*, November 18, 1913; "Nationals Win at Pendleton," *Oregonian*, November 14, 1915, Section Two.

109 "Babes Have Their Inning at Festival," *Oregonian*, May 23, 1913. See also "Roseburg's Great Carnival With Wild West Features is at Hand," *Oregonian*, May 18, 1913, Section Four; "Strawberry King at Roseburg Fete," *Oregonian*, May 22, 1913; "Balloon Trip On," *Oregonian*, May 25, 1913.

110 "Newberg High School Baseball Team Wins 10 of 12 Games Played to Date," *Oregonian*, July 7, 1913 (article includes photo and identifies players); "Salem High Wins Another Contest," *Daily Capital Journal*, June 4, 1913; "Salem Fares Well in Sporting Events," *Daily Capital Journal*, December 20, 1913, Section Three ("The high school baseball team was easily the champion of the state of Oregon").

111 "Nehalem Tigers Victors," *Oregonian*, May 7, 1918.

112 "Salem YMCA Has Team," *Oregonian*, November 18, 1913; "Salem Loses to Silverton," *Oregonian*, November 28, 1913; "Mt. Angel Takes Game from Salem 30 to 29," *Daily Capital Journal*, December 6, 1913.

113 "Montreal Team is Hockey Champion," *Oregonian*, March 31, 1916; "Johnson is Back," *Oregonian*, April 24, 1916; "Uncle Sams Win Opener Here, 2–1," *Oregonian*, December 11, 1915.

114 "Oregon Eyed by Fans," *Oregonian*, November 27, 1922.

115 "Los Angeles Takes Six Games," *Oregonian*, May 29, 1916 (Claxton appeared in both games of a double header and is listed in the box score as Klaxton).

116 "Newberg 39, Forest Grove 15," *Oregonian*, January 31, 1914; "Newberg Claims Title," *Oregonian*, March 8, 1914, Section Two; "M'Minnville Team is Victor," *Oregonian*, March 22, 1914, Section Two; "Right to Title of Basketball Championship of State Asserted," *Oregonian*, April 2, 1914.

117 "Salem Defeats Eugene," *Oregonian*, November 15, 1914, Section Two; "Willamette is Leader," *Oregonian*, November 21, 1915, Section Two.

118 *Oregonian*, August 30, 1921. This photo appeared in the *Oregonian* in 1916 with a caption indicating Dewey was running for the Multnomah Amateur Athletic Club. See "Quintet of Athletes Who Will Vie for Honors in the Far Western Indoor Track and Field Championships at Corvallis, Or. Next Saturday Afternoon," *Oregonian*, March 26, 1916, Section Two.

119 "Beavers Stronger, Says Rube Foster," *Oregonian*, April 2, 1915; "Recruit Pitchers Beat Black Team," *Oregonian*, March 22, 1915; "Chinese is Not to Join Beaver Team," *Oregonian*, December 27, 1914, Section Two.

120 "Arlington to Celebrate Fourth," *Oregonian*, June 29, 1915.

121 "Oregon Is Winner In Sea of Mud, 9–0," *Oregonian*, November 21, 1915.

122 "Clatskanie High School Baseball Team Closes Year Undefeated," *Oregonian*, June 4, 1916. The *Oregonian* article included this same photo with player identifications.

123 "Fast Team Lined Up," *Oregonian*, March 22, 1916; "St. Helens Lose Two Games," *St. Helens Mist*, June 2, 1916 (the *St. Helens Mist* article included this same Kirkpatricks photo, but without player identifications. For a different photo of the Kirkpatricks team with players identified, see "This Aggregation is Tied With the Bradfords for the Leadership of the Inter-City Baseball League," *Oregonian*, May 7, 1916, Section Two; "Final Games Today," *Oregonian*, August 27, 1916, Section Two.

124 "Defenders of Prineville's Base Ball Honor," *Crook County Journal*, September 7, 1916 (article includes a different photo of the Prineville team, with players identified); "Aeroplane Flights," *Crook County Journal*, September 14, 1916 ("Baseball Championship Series Will be Played During the Fair for the Championship of the State between Prineville and the Baby Beavers"); "Prineville Captures Title," *Oregonian*, September 25, 1916; "Baby Beavers to Seek Title," *Oregonian*, September 27, 1916; "Baby Beavers Win 4 Straight Games," *Crook County Journal*, October 5, 1916.

125 "Columbia Club Football Team, of Astoria, Or., Undefeated Champions of Lower Columbia," *Oregonian*, December 10, 1916, Section Two. The article included this same photo with players identified. The hero of the game, Larson, is identified in the text as Leo and in the caption as Leon—which name is correct is unknown.

126 "University Athletes Planning to Return," *Oregonian*, January 5, 1919, Section Two (identifying Gamble as having been a freshmen baseball player in 1918). The University of Oregon yearbook *Oregana* identifies him as a member of the varsity team in 1919, 1920, and 1921. For his receiving letters in sports, see "U. of O. Men Get Sweaters," *Oregonian*, July 10, 1919; "Fourteen Oregon Warriors Get O," *Oregon City Enterprise*, February 13, 1920.

127 "Money Changers are Undefeated," *Oregon Statesman*, February 28, 1918.

128 "Oregon is Victor Over Hardy O.A.C.," *Oregonian*, November 16, 1919.

129 "Jefferson Finishes With Clean Slate," *Oregonian*, November 25, 1919; "Jefferson High School Football Team Which Copped Interscholastic Title in 1918 and Is Making a Strong Bid Again This Year," *Oregonian*, October 12, 1919, Section Two (article includes the same photo without the ovals and without player identification); "Jefferson High Wins," *Oregonian*, April 23, 1910 (Jefferson vs. Portland Academy); "Lincoln Is Downed," *Oregonian*, May 27, 1910.

130 "Pullman Crushed by Oregon, 13 to 0," *Oregonian*, November 12, 1922, Section Two.

APPENDIX

1 No record of an 1867 Corvallis team was found, but the *Oregon City Enterprise* reported that the *Gazette* (presumably the *Corvallis Gazette*) had suggested to "the young men of Corvallis the propriety of organizing a base ball club. It would afford a healthful and pleasant pastime" (*Oregon City Enterprise*, June 8, 1867, Oregon).

2   The *Oregonian* did not identify this team
     by name so it may be one of the Salem clubs
     appearing elsewhere on this list. Without
     evidence that is the case, it is listed separately.
     Probably the most definitive statement on
     1867 Salem baseball clubs comes in the July 22
     entry—by that date Salem had eight teams.

3   The article stated that the *"Journal"* (likely
     the *Albany Journal*) said an Albany team "will
     be formed." It presumably was formed so it is
     included here. However, an Albany newspaper
     reported in September 1867 that the "'young
     bloods' of this city" had failed to form a base-
     ball club ("Base Ball," *State Rights Democrat*,
     September 7, 1867). Cities often had adult and
     young adult teams known as juveniles. The
     reference to "young bloods" may refer to the
     latter, and if so it would not contradict the June
     4 article if that indeed pertained to an adult
     team. A Web-foot team had formed in Albany
     by 1868 ("Base Ball," *State Rights Democrat*,
     June 27, 1868).

4   The article added that the team had ad-
     opted the name and costume of the Scotch
     Highlanders. The club's early records are at
     the Oregon Historical Society (reference Call
     Number Mss 317).

5   For reference to the team name Dysodia, see
     "Base Ball," *Oregon State Journal*, July 13, 1867.

6   The *Oregonian* identified a Pacific team from
     Portland on September 17, 1867, but the Pacific
     team that played the Willamette Club was a
     different team and hailed from Salem. See the
     Oregonian, July 16, 1867, State Items (describ-
     ing the Pacific Club by reference to Salem's
     Commercial Street).

7   The Willamette club is identified as being from
     Willamette University (*Oregonian*, July 16,
     1867, State Items).

8   The article from the July 25, 1867 *Oregonian*
     states that Salem had eight baseball clubs.
     Three Salem teams appear on this list of clubs
     up until that date, so a general reference has
     been included here about the other five.

9   The article spelled the team name using a
     hyphen (Clear-Away). A later article spelled it
     as one word and is assumed to have corrected
     the earlier spelling ("Juvenile Match Game,"
     Oregonian, August 10, 1867, City).

10   The newspaper also stated that as of August 1
     there were eleven baseball clubs in Portland.
     The Appendix identifies seven clubs from
     the city as having been organized before that
     date. As for the other four clubs, perhaps
     some have not been uncovered, or some ap-
     pearing later in the Appendix were organized
     earlier, or both ("Later," *Oregonian*, August 1,
     1867, City).

11   "The Phull-Phellers. – A T.B. club [B.B. for
     "baseball" was likely the intended abbrevia-
     tion, one commonly used at that time] of this
     name has been organized, and, we learn, will
     play a game at one o'clock this afternoon on the
     Pioneer's grounds. We suspect there will be
     phun."

12   The Spartan Base Ball Club organized on
     August 26, according to that article. An August
     1 date is given in the *Portland Directory for the
     year commending January 1868* (20), but the
     article is likely correct because of its specificity
     and proximity to the event.

INDEX